SCHOOL SITE BUDGETING

Decentralized School Management

John Greenhalgh

UNIVERSITY
PRESS OF
AMERICA

LANHAM • NEW YORK • LONDON

To Charles W. Fowler,

Inventor/Mentor

TABLE OF CONTENTS

TABLE OF CONTENTS (Continued)

TABLE OF CONTENTS (Continued)

LIST OF TABLES

LIST OF FIGURES

Preface

This book is about a promising approach to the administration of schools and school districts. It may be misleading to give budgeting top billing in the title. It's not another book about school budgeting, laced with theory or accounting rules. Instead, it offers a plan to improve school management by distributing all planning decisions to local school building administrators. The budget acts as a conduit to relay the decisions to the central district governing authority.

The ordinarily centralized pattern of school district management is often slow to accommodate the avowed needs of students, teachers, parents, and school administrators. With this decentralized arrangement, each school decides how to maximize educational opportunities for each member of the school. School building leaders grow in stature as a result of expanded powers of planning and directorship.

Some arguments for this approach include:

Decisions made closest to the students are the best decisions.

Each student should have equal access to educational resources.

Program decisions should be quickly and effectively carried out.

Incentives should be provided for performance.

Community planning input improves school support.

Recent inventions have a profound impact on school management. Such developments as pocket calculators, video cassette recorders, photocopiers, microcomputers, and telecommunication networks tend to support a wholly different relationship between schools and school district central offices. Schools become more independent of the heretofore centralized management structure.

With basics being a pop topic, perhaps this book is really about the basics of a school system administrative relationship - letting the principal again become the principal teacher, principal planner, principal administrator, and principal manager of a school building.

J.G.

Chapter 1

TWO WAYS TO PLAN SCHOOL BUDGETS

The building principal finished filling in the blanks on the budget forms and sent them on to the district central office. It had been easy to complete the uncomplicated forms. Only a few choices were offered: supplies, books and library materials, field trips and extra-curricular activities, repair and replacement of equipment, new personnel and reclassifications, and capital outlay.

Several weeks earlier, the principal had carefully distributed copies of the budget forms and staff members were asked to list their needs for the upcoming year. In varying degrees they responded and provided additional arguments to support their suggestions. The principal assembled the requests and produced the summary request of the school. In two or three months the school would be told how the budget request had faired by the funding levels approved from somewhere within the district administrative office. Allocations would appear as line items within THE budget of the school district. Then the budget lines would be subject to further review and/or change at the time of legislative review.

The principal and staff members found it difficult to trace the logic that caused some of the lower priority items to be funded while some of their more vital needs received reduced funding or were totally overlooked. Somehow they were led to believe that the global review of the central office staff and governing board made balanced decisions in the best interest of the school district. Sometimes it seemed that such decisions produced a program of averaged mediocrity - striving for a middle ground of consensus. The process was not too unlike the natural spawning of fish and the chance survival and maturation of some of the fry.

In a neighboring school district, a very different planning process was taking place. Centrally, a major decision was made establishing the total amount of money available for the operation of the school district. Next, the money was divided into proportionate shares for each type of student of the district. The per pupil allowances were summarized and assigned to the individual school buildings where the students would attend. Each school received a lump sum allocation with which

1

to meet all of the needs of the students. The building principal had a different planning role in that school district; how to get the most value from the available resources. Rather than distribute forms which solicited inocuous data, the planning process became one of discussion, exploration, selection, compromise, and maximizing applications. It involved all the staff members, since without participation their vested interests may not be looked after. Decisions were of sufficient and final magnitude that parents, alumni, and even students became full-share participants in the process. Through all of this, the building principal patiently and tactfully reserved the right to make the final judgement - while being sensitive to each element of the school constituency. Though the dialog was provoked by the need to develop a fiscal plan, the matter of money was quickly overshadowed by consideration of pupil and staff needs and the selection of available alternative options. Key decisions were made in close proximity to the instructional arena.

When they finished, the plan was assembled and sent to the central office. Not only were all the rows and columns accurately summarized, but the accompanying narrative explained the consensus of a large group of persons who had focused on the particular needs of the local group of students.

The central office staff made an overall review of the submission, looking for oversights. Mostly, the review was intended to confirm that the building plan would meet the publicized goals of the district and would conform to local, state, and federal statutes.

The individual school budgets were next assembled into a comprehensive plan for the district and exposed for legislative consideration. The superintendent noted that hundreds or even thousands of community members had developed the plan, and it reflected their dynamic recommendations for the next year's school program.

The Making of Large and Small Decisions

Within schools, decentralized decisions making is commonplace. Building leaders are sensitive to staff and student concerns and incorporate their participation in planning activities, whether it be a simple decision such as affixing the date of the annual picnic or a complex decision regarding the scheduling, group-

2

ing, or sequential arrangement of instructional activities. Wide participation occurs in developing enrichment activities (assemblies, field trips, sports, music, drama, literary, etc.) and in planning for the management of classroom learning activities. In general, the critical matters of student growth and development are largely left to local building autonomy, acting within the broadest system-wide policies and generalized administrative regulations. The "how and when" elements of instruction are customarily relegated to the administrative level of school buildings.

But, typically, the "who" (personnel), and "what" (curriculum texts and materials), and "why" (learning objectives) are reserved to a remote and centralized administrative structure, assuming that greater insight and district-wide perspective are essential ingredients for successful instructional programs. Conformity is accomplished through such activities as staff procurement and assignment, curriculum planning and district-wide text adoptions, and rigidly prescribed centralized budget planning and expenditure control processes.

Just as a chain is only as strong as its weakest link, centralized decisions are only as valid as their weakest assumption. A bad or poor decision has universal impact on the schools of the district.

A strong centralized administrative structure may yet offer some advantages to a school district. Centralized control incorporates detailed planning routines, the promulgation of standards, and uniformity of reporting and control of resource inputs. Consensus is achieved through the use of inter-office memoranda and procedure manuals, highly structured curriculum guides, a regular meeting schedule, and a daily or weekly report process.

In theory, a centralized administrative structure can efficiently and effectively control the educational enterprise within the district. A few well placed commands are supposed to spread throughout the district in a ripple effect. However, ripples only remain concentric on unencumbered planes. Any rigid object will break the ripple effect - and such often occurs in a centrally managed enterprise. Separate building leaders, equally trained and professionally proficient, may make differing interpretations of the centrally provided directive, thus altering the ripple effect. Carrying out of directives may be influenced by a lack of clarity in specification, an adjustment to meet local circumstances, a general foot dragging from unpopular actions, a desire to improve the central efforts, or even a matter of local building leaders applying greater expertise and experience to arrive at a different course of action.

There are some organizations where rigidly centralized administration is state of the art: prisons, military units, marching bands, state run lotteries, and some fast food franchises. But in a social enterprise such as a school district, greater effectiveness can be realized through delegation, participation, pooling and sharing, and by capitalizing on the initiative of persons and groups being administered.

A prime example of the effectiveness of decentralized decision making in a school system is the sports program. Each building establishes local self-contained teams. Great effort is put forth with little regard to the actual or perceived capabilities of the players. There is interest, effort, motivation, and optimism! The athletic appetite overcomes matters of cost, facilities, and scheduling constraints. On the field or court, exemplary individual instruction is provided and there is much evidence of lasting carry-over values among the participants. The decentralized sports program engenders a high degree of (local) community support, indentification, and pride of ownership.

All of this occurs with little centralized regulatory effort. Some limits have been imposed concerning player eligibility, the qualification of coaches, rule modifications to recognize the health and safety of youthful participants, and an appelate process for resolving disputes. But otherwise, each school is autonomous in carrying out a sports program.

There are many reasons why decentralized decision making within a school district is an idea whose time has come. It has to do with personal involvement rather than a collective approach to career development. Child advocacy is marked ahead of bureaucratic efficiency. The movement was significantly helped by the courts in at least 20 states which have recently ruled that their financial support of education must be channeled to provide equal educational opportunities for all students within the state. Simultaneously, the public has become more involved with local school issues, promoting emphasis on basic instruction, and providing extra services to accommodate the special needs of minority groups that need to catch up with the mainstream of society.

Developments in technology also lead to the creation of autonomous management of school buildings. Whereas a school district once may have required centralized support facilities for the production of instructional materials, the development of inexpensive apparatus has enabled point of use production in school buildings: document copiers, cassette recorders, instant photo processing, plastic binding, video cassette recorders, electronic stencil makers, direct offset masters, microcomputers, data terminals, pocket calculators, and word processors. Even if a centralized administrative structure was desired, it would be increasingly difficult to regiment or to monitor the separate school buildings in light of these developments.

School Budgets Are Different

One available means to create a diversified management system is to approach budget planning on a decentralized basis. By relegating the authority for allocation of funds to individual school buildings, a school district can readily and effectively acquire a broadly based planning perspective.

The budget of a school district differs from ordinary commercial, mercantile, or industrial budgets. In the world of business, a budget is an accounting/control device; a forecast to predict outcomes of events. It is results oriented. Whereas in the realm of school budgeting, the emphasis is on being concerned with concepts of human relationships by assigning the resources in advance of performance. A school budget is a device for focusing on the input side of a production model.

In a centrally administered school district, the finalization of a budget is buried deep within a central office accounting complex. In a decentralized school district, the budget of each instructional center is developed by building leaders, staff members, parents, students, and community members, assembling information in a fish bowl atmosphere.

Financial decisions have a profound influence on educational decisions. And, since educational output is not wholly traceable to fiscal input, the cost-benefit relationship is not precise. The amount of resources to be designated for the support of schools is partly a political, sociological, and economic decision.

School systems often have placid governance except for that time of the year when educational allocations are to be set. Few things cause such attention to be paid to schools as the annual school budget hearing. Balanced reason often is supplanted by the emotionalism of fiscal conservatism or liberalism. The major operational decisions of a school system are often adopted as part of a spending package, and frequently as a diluted compromise which partially appeases all factions while wholly satisfying none.

When educational budgeting is decentralized and school building administrators gain the power to make final spending decisions, a significant change takes place in the way schools (and school systems) are managed. Decision making becomes decentralized. This shift of power needs to be understood if the school site budgeting process is to succeed. There is no inherent reason why the school site budgeting process would work best at a given size or configuration of a school district. School site budgeting can occur at a school district composed of one, two, or a hundred separate schools. The only elements to be affected are size related planning assumptions regarding centralized efficiencies of some non-instructional matters. For some volume purchasing considerations, big is beautiful. But for customized educational decisions, small is swell. Such considerations require careful planning in advance of the adoption of school site budgeting techniques.

The matter of deciding which decisions will be retained centrally and which will be consigned to school buildings requires a rational perspective. On the one hand there is the elected or appointed body of school governors, charged with the care, custody, and control of the school system. On the other hand are the professional administrators of a school unit, charged with effectively carrying out the policies of the governing board. It is necessary to select the best instructional alternatives from a set of feasible and available strategies and to assign the required funding to purchase the components. Where is the most expert judgement for such decisions? Most likely it is at the building level where more is known about the peculiarities of the learners and the complex amalgam of attitudes, values, and norms that are housed within each building. Discussions of centralization or decentralization must consider the premise and promise of school site budgeting; to more exactly meet the classroom needs of teachers and learners.

There is the potential for improved responsiveness at the consumer level. Parents are most apt to get their childrens' academic, emotional, or maturation problems satisfied by a visit to a school than by detailing their needs to the downtown superintendent. It would work the same way with other governmental units such as requesting to a letter carrier that the mail be delivered to a side door in place of a front door, or in asking the local patrolman to help prevent children from straying into roadways. In both cases, a centralized and remote bureaucrat would be slower to achieve the desired results.

Some decisions regarding the operation of schools can better be made centrally; those which require a degree of uniformity for purposes of efficiency, economy, or understanding. Such decisions would include those of closing schools when weather conditions dictate, uniform wage scales and employee benefits, compliance with statutory requirements, master labor agreements, resource entitlements, accounting and reporting, and matters of public welfare and relationship to other governmental agencies. Centrally retained decisions must also have some input from school building administrators if they are to succeed. Note that all of the above are not related to the daily classroom instructional agenda, but are important.

The Administrative Change

Determining which powers are to be exercised within a central administrative structure or relinquished to schools requires some early philosophical and/or political determinations. It is not unlike the problem encountered two hundred years ago when separate colonies were banding together as a larger political entity. Some concerns were decentralized to the states: education, public roads, state courts, licensing, public records (real estate), while others were retained at the federal level: defense, inter-

7

national relations, patent protection, coinage, and mail service. And, there is found to be considerable overlapping in many other state-federal governmental relations: taxation, preserving 'public peace, agriculture, law making, natural resources, and the regulation of commerce. Whenever several levels of management take place, but especially at multiple sites, it is essential that the degrees of autonomy are established, understood, and constantly subject to review and upgrading.

How then can centrally administered school districts come to grips with the ideological basis of decentralizing a budgetary process? Try this! The governing board (of education) decides WHAT is to be done and WHY it is important. The central administrator (the superintendent) decides WHO is to do it and WHERE it is to be done. The local building administrator then decides HOW it is to be accomplished and in so doing faces the contingent problem of WHEN.

In determining the WHAT and WHY of education, the board establishes policies concerned with very long range goals. Examples might include the grade levels when foreign languages are offered or the requirements for high school graduation. In so doing, the board will, through debate, explore WHY such policies are to be adopted. Note that board goals are framed in terms of the very broadest concepts. There can be little question that the destinations of the schools are centrally established at this level.

Next, the superintendent of schools has the job of putting the board's goals into practice. Through subordinate administrators the issues of WHERE actions are to occur and WHO will carry them out are decided. Such decisions as the number and grade levels and make-up of school units are decisions primarily made by the central administrative structure. System wide labor negotiations concerned with the WHO aspects of educational staffing are of necessity reserved as a centralized responsibility in order to prevent a whip-sawing effect of competitively fragmented labor practices.

In a reasonably decentralized school district decisions of HOW (and WHEN) instruction is to be accomplished are made at the local building level - closest to where such decisions are carried out. In

8

order to reach for the board's instructional goals, local building leaders must be given a sufficient degree of autonomy, authority, and control of their domestic operation. The federal constitution gives the states all powers not specifically retained at the federal level. A decentralized school system must give the schools all the powers not specifically retained at the central administrative level. The local assignment of decision making must include adequate authority to control the factors affecting locally made decisions.

Decentralized authority provides a multiplicity of judgements and tends to avoid a single bias. Some decisions must be shared by local and centralized administrators.

The element of quality control of the educational process is the kind of a major concern that both levels cannot overlook. Program evaluation and pupil progress are the basic yardsticks of output of a school and a school district. The origin of instructional decisions is also the location for initial evaluation of such decisions.

Another shared decision element would be that of allocation of money. Since all three levels of governance have some financial decisions reserved for their domain, there must be a good amount of coordination of financial decision making.

From an administrative viewpoint, the issue of decentralized school operations requires a lot of confidence in subordinate administrators. Where many persons are making more decisions on a smaller scale, it is likely that the errors in judgement will be smaller and affect a narrower range of activities. Confidence implies that occasional failures can be accommodated without catastrophic results, retributions, or damage to the decentralization process. The rewards of providing creative individual solutions to on-going problems outweigh the disadvantages of occasional redundancy or oversight.

Aside from occasional errors, the administrative advantages of decentralized decision making are plentiful. Building level administrators possess a peculiar perspective to educational problems. Their role has been one of taking direction from a higher administrative echelon and skillfully implementing those requirements with subordinate instructional staff members. In so doing, their imprimatur is affixed. But is that enough, or are there particular contributions to be made at building level administration? While centralized decision making provides system-wide perspective, the chief advantage of decentralized decision making is one of school site perspective; in the trenches. Something may be lost in translation when building level problems are transmitted for adjudication to a remote (higher) level. In providing universal (system wide) responses to local building concerns, a centralized power base tends to "average" solutions to discrete concerns. The best fit is not always achieved.

An obvious question is where can such decisions best be made? The term "best" refers to maximum instructional advantage. School site budgeting places instructional decisions at the school building level, close to the arena. This is apt to require more time and planning by building administrators, but such efforts will produce more satisfying decisions. There's a self fulfilling prophecy inherent when persons are carrying out activities which they had a part in deciding.

Building level administrators must be totally supported in the process of arriving at instructional (and spending) decisions. Unless complete protection is afforded, often through pre-auditing of plans, people will not assume risks which could lead to their demise or embarrassment. The central administrative structure must provide guide lines for local autonomous decisions. Such guide lines must be applied in broad brush strokes and not as a rigid outline designed for building administrators to color within the lines. If the right degree of assurance, security, guidance, and supportive service is provided, there will be a purge of local administrative lethargy. But there needs to be a high degree of consistency in the relationship between a central administrative structure and a building level administrative structure. Accountability auditing will only be successful so long as sensitivity to local conditions is practiced. Decentralization of school administration is a total process, not a sometimes thing.

The Instructional Change

Decentralization facilitates experimentation. Differing instructional methods, materials, staffing, time blocks, and pupil-teacher relationships are often tried out within a school building in an effort to better meet specified instructional objectives. Children learn from their immediate environment. Decentralization permits and demands the manipulation of instructional stimuli. Each student is slightly different and will react in a differing manner. A variety of flexible teaching activities is needed to give each child a program to best meet his/her requirements at a given point in time. Decisions (decentralized) are made on a timely basis.

Students are subjected to normal human behavior variability in moods, attitudes, and physical health. To accommodate such daily diversification it is necessary that the educational program be adapted to the current state of the learners. Such one on one flexibility would be virtually impossible to achieve if a highly structured and rigid centralized curriculum were to be imposed on a district wide basis. Yet, in the past such scope and sequence learning activities have been adopted as a centrally rendered judgement. Individual differences were only accommodated by the pace (for slower learners) or embellishment (for faster learners) of THE curriculum. A whole concept of responsiveness (to individual needs) was lacking. Simultaneously, little was left to the professional prerogatives of trained and able teachers. Curriculum guides were tolerated rather than transcended. Centralized controls stifled local initiative, especially when deviations were suspect.

When administered on a decentralized basis, each school develops its own production function. While school plans may be pre-audited by a central review authority, such surveillance is intended to help bring system wide resources to the school building. Schools are encouraged to instigate new and creative participation in the achievement of instructional objectives. Their achievements and accomplishments are more easily monitored and measured at the level of a school building, a grade, or even a classroom. Such evaluative criteria are apt to be very applicable due to their small size basis and their timely generation. The strengths and skills of staff members are best exploited by permitting and encouraging their practice on an

11

individual basis. The reader is reminded that the best (instructional presentation) is what is sought through the process of letting instructional decisions be made at a grass roots level. ʹ

The Financial Change

Decentralized budgeting creates decentralized instructional decisions. The budget parcels out and assigns the resources in a locally prescribed manner. Typically a centralized school budget is a control device. It purports to specify precisely what is to be expended and for what purpose. Only those things mentioned in the budget are normally to be carried out. Deviations, transfers, or alterations to spending plans normally require a second round of policy making review. Centrally formulated budgets provide rigid adherence to centrally perceived expenditure plans. As such, they are extremely inflexible. Arguments for decentralized budgetary decisions cite advantages of flexibility and adaptability to pupils' ever changing needs. P. T. Barnum once described money as a terrible master but an excellent servant.

When schools are to be governed with the aid of decentralized budgetary decisions, they achieve a high level of fiscal independence. With such privilege comes the concordant requirement for uniform accounting and reporting requirements. The element of public trust and confidence can best be served by the universal application of sound managerial techniques. Tests of comparability cannot be made if each unit utilizes a differing accounting base. In a sense, the critical review of expenditure patterns is re-directed from the central administrative unit to a school building administrative unit. As earlier implied, with rights come responsibilities. One such responsibility is the assurance of a continuous flow of current information concerning local building level operations. Modern data processing capability is a prerequisite for developing workable decentralized budgeting processes. The pulse of the patient requires the continuous monitoring of a drone-like data processing facility. Decisions are best made on the basis of facts. While a degree of intuitive judgement is ever present, the competitive edge must go to the person with the greater degree of hard knowledge. Decentralization causes a sunburst of smaller decisions in place of lethargic major decisions. The only financial decisions to be justifiably retained at the central administrative office are those (1) that do not directly affect the teaching-learning process, (2) with an inherent capability of producing efficient, large scale financial economies, or (3) having system wide application as a result of imposed statutes or contractual agreements, or (4) overall cut-backs imposed by budget cutting review agencies.

In dealing with public monies, there is always a requirement for openness, accountability, prudence, sound planning, and independent auditing. To meet these conditions, the decentralization process needs a planned structure. Measures of comparability can only be applied to data assembled in standard formats. Yet, within the rigidity of a recording and reporting system there must be provision for capitalizing on the largest advantage of decentralized operation: adaptability to local needs. This can be accomplished by a process that accommodates structured transfer of funds or realignment of allocated funds. Safeguards would insist that such financial shifts be well planned, visibly executed, and decided on such logical bases as shifting enrollments, changes in program emphases, staff replacements, new technology or method, unforseeable circumstances, or changes brought about through relationship with other parts of school operations.

Decentralized budgeting forges the available dollars into precision parts, customized to fit specific tactical needs. Conversely, centralized budgeting assigns funds on a gross scale, hoping to responsibly accommodate average requirements in the manner of a strategic support service. By carefully chosing the level at which budgetary decisions are to be rendered, it is possible to incorporate both strategies in a planned and structured fashion. If, for example, a school district were to acquire basic supply items, (paper, writing instruments, paints and crayons, paste, rulers, scissors, etc.) purchased in economical volume quantities and stockpiled, they would be efficiently provided for all school buildings in a centralized fashion. It is assumed that average quality, size, and type materials would be made available in this manner. School buildings as an adjunct, would have some assigned monies for the purchase of specialized school supplies to best suit their exact needs. Examples of their similar but special supply needs would be art papers and foils, calligraphy pens, epoxy cements, acrylic paints, machinist scales, pinking shears, etc.. With proper planning, centralized and decentralized school financial

13

involvements can be integrated.

Decentralized budgeting provides a variety of decisions affecting instructional expenditures. There's an inherent efficiency in the marketplace resulting from decentralized spending decisions. Mistakes are small and individual in nature. Only the individual purchaser is adversely affected. Too little will be spent on some items and too much will be spent on others. Some decisions will be more efficacious than others. What errors do take place will affect a small number of students - whereas an expansive response from a centralized station can provide errors of immense magnitude. A tenet of democracy is that many decisions are better than one!

The Political Change

Of all the fall-out from decentralizing the management of a school system, the aspects of political control may be the most difficult to rationalize. The pressures (real or implied) for obedience, dependency, or conformity must instantly vanish. The security of a well oiled bureaucratic buffer system is not available when decisions are truly made at independent school sites. That is precisely "where the buck stops". In practice, however, it would not be desirable to create such a changeover instantly. Since the luxury of time and pre-planning are available, it would be reasonable to promote an orderly transition from dependency on centralized authority to autonomous building level functioning.

Benson[1] revealed some of the complexity of understanding the political ramifications of decentralizing the management of public affairs.

> "What is the case for local government? And what is the case for local control of schools? It is interesting that the general view of local government appears to split along party lines in a certain paradoxical way. The Democratic party finds acceptable a greater centralization in public activities, by and large, but is extremely wary of centralization in private activities. The Republican party is a staunch advocate of local government but accepts the consequences of large scale business enterprise."

14

Fortunately the compartmentalization of political thought is not precisely achieved. Gradations permit the development of local logic, timely rationalization, and grass roots agreements concerning the administration and management of schools and school systems.

When transferring administrative powers from central control to individual school buildings, a clearly understood policy is essential. This must include the committment and conviction of top level leadership and policy makers as well as the acceptance and understanding of the persons to whom the power is to be granted. Mostly broad issues remain at a central level and specific issues are best relegated to a school level. Previous educational writers have described and illustrated such relationships in the form of a pyramid with the Board of Education and superintendent of schools at the narrow tip and the schools fanned out along the base. In decentralized operation, the pyramid might be inverted, with the Board of Education being concerned with a wide range, long term, all encompassing guidance concern and the school/s being at the saw tooth tips as the agents to the task of instruction in a day to day problem solving sphere.

Centralization of school management worked best when the schools had a well defined and universally accepted narrow mission. The few things that were expected to be accomplished were readily identified, easily dispensed, reinforced through endless drill and repetition, and conveniently measured. The schools' roles were to follow the script and effectively infuse the circumscribed body of knowledge. The central administrators and policy makers could prove achievement by precisely measuring the absorption rates of the students. If more vanilla, chocolate, or strawberry was needed, more was pumped in. However, with the explosion of the schools' goals to incorporate an expanded body of knowledge, it became apparent that centrally decreed decisions often were unable to cope with the variety of field problems arising in the schools. Pupils and teachers have sought breadth and relevancy in their school experiences. Rote fact filling was not providing relevancy nor keeping pace with fissioning technology. With easy movements of residences, the former homogeneous neighborhoods or whole communities gave way to newcomers of divergent background. The singular school curriculum no longer mirrored the diverse goals and aspirations of the community. Decentralization of school governance and direction is a response to the need for providing local school programs that are meaningful and right for the consumers - not necessarily administratively tidy - but timely and important.'

When people share in the making of decisions affecting their futurity, there's a sense of added effort towards self fulfillment. There also exists a sustained interest, a continuous and responsive monitoring, and the facility to make changes as required to accomplish identified outcomes.

Political ramifications of decentralizing of school operation will cause tremors in labor relations. Where initially the issues were resolved with a central authority, many such decisions would be relegated to the numerous decision centers in various school buildings. More exceptions and locally devised pragmatic resolution of contractual language will occur. The pressure points for stimulus will be more numerous, less universal, more difficult to assemble, and more responsive, but in a limited field. It could be likened to driving and controlling a large ocean liner with a series of outboard motors. Pressures for obediency and dependency would vanish. They would be replaced by mutually developed respect and response. Power and power relationships would require a whole new set of ground rules. The new balances of power between the governing board, the chief administrative officer and the middle level building administrators would be irreversibly altered.

Thomas Jefferson wrote: "But it is not the consolidation, or concentration, of powers, but by their distribution that good government is effected."

To make decentralization work, several rules of relationships are offered.

1. Be secure and committed. Risk-taking, like mountain climbing, requires solid footing before progress can be achieved.

2. Plan and prepare. Unlike traveling with a credit card "ride now, pay later", decentralized school operations require unqualified preparation. It proposes evolution, not revolution.

16

3. <u>Define limits.</u> Circumscribe the arena within which decisions will be featured. Provide reserved seats for the spectators and a good playing surface for the participants. All contests must be open to the general public.

4. <u>Explain consequences.</u> Let each decision maker know how the score (evaluation) is to be kept. Participants should know in advance what back-up or fail-safe resources will (and will not) be available to support their decisions.

5. <u>Do and re-do it.</u> Most discoveries are made after some trial and error, even though the final goal was always paramount. Be prepared to make mid-course corrections.

6. <u>Audit.</u> If it's worth doing, it should be measurable or at least observable. If it's measurable, it's important. If it's important, identify it.

   Why decentralize the administration of a school system? To have more people try harder to provide classroom delivery of the most appropriate instructional program to each student.

1. Charles S. Benson, <u>The Economics of Public Education</u>, (Boston: Houghton Mifflin Co., 1961), p. 226.

Chapter 2

EDUCATIONAL EQUALITY

Decentralized decision making provides each student with an EQUAL chance of experiencing the best educational program a community can provide. The availability of equivalent educational opportunities was mandated by the landmark school finance court decision: Serrano vs Priest. The judicial authority determined that the financing of education in California (by property taxes) violated the Fourteenth Amendment to the Constitution and "invidiously discriminates against the poor because it makes the quality of a child's education a function of the wealth of his parents and neighbors".[1]

The Fourteenth Amendment to the Constitution specifies, "No state shall ... deny to any person within its jurisdiction the equal protection of the laws".

Similar court findings have successfully challenged unequal funding for schools in Texas, New Jersey, Arizona, Wyoming, Kansas, Michigan, Connecticut, and a dozen other states. Most states have a system of scattering financial assistance for local schools without regard to the financial ability or the willingness of a community to support educational services. Property rich communities tend to make greater expenditures for school purposes, while property poor communities are unable to provide corresponding educational opportunities. Each community gets significant financial support from state school funding formulas that ignore such disparity. Providing equal aid to communities of unequal need tends to perpetuate inequality. There is a need to develop equitable school funding systems to deliver full scale educational services to each pupil.

All Things Being Equal

Not only schools, but a host of governmental concerns have been caught up in the trend to accommodate the needs of individuals. The Equal Employment Opportunity Act has added a new dimension to the implementation of affirmative action hiring plans. Title VII of the Civil Rights Act of 1964 bars discrimination in employment on the basis of race, color, sex, religion, or national origin, and its provisions are enforced by the Equal Employment Opportunity Commission. Title IX of the Education Amendments of 1972 foster myriad activities in opening new vistas of equality for female persons. The Fair Labor Standards Act of 1938, as amended, specifies that equal wages be paid for equal work without regard to the gender of employees. Section 504 of the Rehabilitation Act of 1973, as amended, provides equal access to public buildings by handicapped persons. The massive legislative reapportionment of the past decade was brought about by the drive for equal (one person, one vote) representation of the electorate. And, electioneering campaigns generated a requirement for availability of equal media time for all bona fide candidates. The seminal concept of equality is an idea whose time has come.

It has taken 200 years to apply to schools the expressed intent of the signers of the Declaration of Independence, "We hold these truths to be self evident, that all men are created equal ...". The present awareness might be linked to the awakening of a concern for minority groups, as in Brown vs The Board of Education of Topeka.[2] Here the judicial system found that "separate but equal" schooling was inherently unequal.

Social mobility is often an outgrowth of educational attainment which leads to improved employment and earnings. The outcome of the Brown decision is to require a single educational system within a community, available to all persons regardless of their chance personal characteristics or socio-economic classification.

Though untested in the courts, a like analysis might reveal a basic inequity at the interstate level insofar as school funding has occurred, Table 2-1 shows the varying expenditures for public elementary and secondary education on a per pupil basis. Spending for education produces a disparity of 3.5 between the highest (Alaska) and the lowest (Mississippi) states.

It is not easy to equate educational burdens on an interstate basis. Some cost variations would be attributed to climate (with added heating or cooling costs), some variations would be caused by a geographical position (with differing shipping costs), while others would be modified by natural resources and the prevailing economic climate. Population sparsity or

20

Table 2.1 Expenditure per pupil in average daily attendance in public elementary and secondary schools, by State: 1980-81

United States $2,701

Alabama	$1,936	Missouri	$2,395
Alaska	6,343	Montana	3,036
Arizona	2,601	Nebraska	2,748
Arkansas	1,954	Nevada	2,496
California	2,547	New Hampshire	2,429
Colorado	3,110	New Jersey	3,595
Connecticut	2,759	New Mexico	2,555
Delaware	3,312	New York	3,970
Dist. of Columbia	3,459	North Carolina	2,149
Florida	2,526	North Dakota	2,192
Georgia	1,986	Ohio	2,479
Hawaii	2,809	Oklahoma	2,484
Idaho	2,155	Oregon	3,473
Illinois	2,915	Pennsylvania	3,007
Indiana	2,327	Rhode Island	3,075
Iowa	2,569	South Carolina	2,183
Kansas	2,517	South Dakota	2,229
Kentucky	1,954	Tennessee	1,979
Louisiana	2,245	Texas	2,410
Maine	2,129	Utah	2,299
Maryland	3,241	Vermont	2,450
Massachusetts	3,070	Virginia	2,401
Michigan	2,874	Washington	3,310
Minnesota	2,997	West Virginia	2,395
Mississippi	1,784	Wisconsin	2,935
		Wyoming	3,756

Includes current expenditures for day schools, capital outlay, and interest on school debt.

SOURCE: U.S. Department of Education, National Center for Education Statistics, preliminary data from the survey of "Common Core of Data."

density would affect school costs by the relative savings or burdens of larger or smaller pupil populations. The very purchasing power of the dollar in each state would require analysis prior to a meaningful comparison of interstate efforts. Yet even with all these qualifications, most states can relate to their "yardstick" neighbors for purposes of comparing income, expenditures, and school support statistics.

The equalization of educational opportunity is not a simple accomplishment. Note the comparison offered by Shannon:[3]

> "It must be admitted that those who draft model equalization legislation have something in common with the race horse handicapper. To use the parlance of the race track, we dream of that day when all school districts will finish in a very fast dead heat. This utopian vision assumes, of course, that we can all agree on the standard for measuring performance and that we can control or compensate for the pace of each entry in a diverse field.
>
> In the real world, there is something less than universal agreement about performance standards, and the race horse handicapper and the educational equalizer must employ very different means to achieve their financial equalization objectives. The handicapper attempts to equalize the race by imposing heavier burdens on the more fleet of hoof. School equalization advocates seek to narrow the gap between the rich and the poor school districts by providing greater financial spur to the poorer districts.
> (The) equalization plan is designed to insure that all districts leave the starting gate at the same time."

Were schools more like manufacturing concerns, the product would be of equal size, shape, and quality. A manufacturer controls not only the processing and fabrication of goods, but more importantly, controls the uniformity of the raw materials. Schools, or at least public schools, must accept an extremely divergent array of students expecting educational processing and fabrication. The best that can be hoped for is that equal opportunities will be provided to enable each child to get the maximum benefits of being taught and of experiencing the utmost educational program. The program must be both proffered and promoted.

State Funding Schemes

Shortly after 1900, many states were providing funds for local school support. Ellwood P. Cubberly was an early theoretician of financial aid for school purposes. He was committed to equality of educational opportunity but his theories tended to provide added funds to those school districts which already provided extended programs - a reward for effort. Yet, he wrote "The duty of the state is to ... equalize the (instructional) advantages to all as nearly as can be done with the resources at hand".[4]

After 1923, the report of the Educational Finance Inquiry Commission of the schools of New York sought to better equalize education by means of a foundation or minimal program grant - the famous Strayer-Haig studies. Many such state plans for financial assistance for school funding are still intact.

Recently some states have switched to an open-ended system of school finance wherein a rate of assistance is created but without a ceiling or expenditure limitation. Such permissive funding choices have had the effect of creating a gap between those communities that have sponsored high cost schools and those others who have provided minimal cost schools, most often because of available tax income. Those fiscal disparities have prompted considerable review and analysis of the issue of providing equivalent educational opportunities for all children of a state.

Each of the three levels of school governing structures has the inherent problem of establishing a semblance of equality. Although education is constitutionally a state function, the infusion of federal funding cannot help but acknowledge the interstate disparities of educational expenditures. To reduce such incongruence might prove to be a difficult task. The very geographical and climatic dispersion would require sophisticated statistical treatment.

The intrastate variations of school expenditures

are being attacked in most states, but with a great deal of difficulty. Problem issues include the redistribution of wealth, an urban - suburban disparity of purchasing power, local control of schools, and the issue of levelling up or levelling down of school districts at opposing spectral poles.

Intradistrict equality is most likely the easiest to accomplish. An accessible and locally responsive school board is best able to decree meaningful efforts to achieve parity throughout the district. The impediments to such efforts would include historic inertia, extant labor agreements, uninspired leadership, and the absence of methodology, (all of which can be readily overcome if equality of effort is to be transfused to the level of the individual pupil).

One of the earliest efforts to deal with comparability studies of financial inputs on a basis close to the student level would be the requirements for proving "comparability" of costs among the schools of a district as a requirement for ESEA funding, Title I. Again, there is the assumption that expenditures and educational opportunities have a fairly direct relationship.

The Neighborhood Bias

Getting the dollars to the school districts on an equalized basis will not insure that each pupil will get a proportionate allocation within the district. Pupils are assigned to neighborhood schools. This tends to batch students according to their dwelling place, which in itself connotes a likeness of economic status. Residences tend to cluster according to economic value: high, middle, and low income housing. Seldom do the three strata mix in a heterogeneous array. Neighborhood schools were designed to reflect the needs of their clients and in so doing, may have perpetuated neighborhood inequality in the support level of the school. Economically successful and well educated parents have provided extra time, talent, interest, and financial donations to assure high level neighborhood schools. Conversely, less educated or inarticulate persons of lower socio-economic neighborhoods lack the time, talent, predisposition, and financial resources to spark increased school efforts in their neighborhood schools. Many years of development of neighborhood schools have extended the disparities between expenditure levels. All citizens of the school district, who pay the same tax rate or extend equivalent efforts in behalf of education should receive services of equal quality and quantity. The level of educational effort is too important to be left to the accident of neighborhood housing configurations. It is not enough to assure a "minimum" or foundation level of support. The efforts must produce an equality of educational opportunity for all pupils.

A study by Sanford[5] examined the variations in cost of education among attendance centers in a large high school district in California. He found a wide range of costs based on student electives, age and size of buildings, and remedial requirements of lower socio-economic clientele. The district did not provide equal per-capita expenditures among the school buildings. Moreover, the study confirmed the presence of a wide range of socio-economic conditions associated with the varying school attendance centers.

In another study, Conant[6] concluded: "The contrast in the money spent per pupil in wealthy suburban schools and in slum schools of the large cities challenges the concept of equality of opportunity in American public education."

Expenditures In - Education Out

In seeking to provide the same educational opportunities, the search generally focuses on the input side of the educational process: money, staff, materials, facilities, and delivery systems. These kind of finite criteria are more easily measurable than the output side of the educational process: understandings, attitudes, achievements, skills, behavioral modifications, experiences, and overall growth and development. It's not yet possible to determine how these outcomes are affected by extraneous forces such as native ability, home environment, peer group relationships, health and self-motivation.

Input elements, on the other hand, can have a price tag attached for ready economic analysis. Hence, the first step towards equalizing educational opportunities most often involves a look towards financial support efforts. There have been notable efforts to provide school funding on an equitable basis to each school district - but not without problems, failures, unequalizing activities (counter-intended), and duplicity.

School Site Budgeting - The New Hope

One emerging idea that offers hope of fulfillment of equalization achievements is a process of school site budgeting. Each school is provided an amount of resources equivalent to the numbers and kinds of students enrolled. Expenditure decisions are made at the building level but must be consistent with district-wide policies and regulations including achievement of specified learning objectives. Expenditures must also accommodate prevailing labor agreements affecting district personnel and wage requirements.

Many school districts have allowed building level discretion on the typical 2% of the building's budget that is set aside for supplies, books, and materials. Too often the tough staffing decisions have been reserved as a central office responsibility or at least a prerogative. Seldom, however, did the goods and commodities purchasing options result in an improvement in rendering school services on a customized basis. Generally a district "adoption" would prescribe the limited range of materials to be acquired. Items were mostly standardized and uniform.

IF EQUAL MATERIALS ARE PURCHASED DISTRICT-WIDE AND DISPENSED EQUALLY TO YOUNGSTERS OF UNEQUAL NEEDS, A PERPETUATION OF INEQUALITY IS FOSTERED. EQUALITY OF OPPORTUNITY DEMANDS THAT THE UNEQUAL NEEDS OF STUDENTS BE MET WITH EQUALLY UNEQUAL EDUCATIONAL RESPONSES!!!

A look at the components of a school district reveals many historical and extant harbingers of inherent inequality between school buildings.

The Differing School Plants

It is rare to find carbon copies of school buildings. As school districts grew, new buildings were erected. Some communities have school buildings that span more than a 75 year period of construction. That phenomena causes a divergence of features, flexibility, program accommodation, and levels of overall efficiency. The buildings have significantly differing upkeep and operational costs and provide varying degrees of comfort to their occupants. Specialized facilities for comprehensive educational programs are sometimes limited by the age and condition of the school plant. The grounds surrounding a school building are seldom similar in size, scope, adaptability, or degree of development. The educational and recreational contributions of school sites are frequently limited by the encroaching development of neighborhood properties.

The Differing Students

Accepting all comers, the public schools provide services to a diverse student population. Differences in personality, cultural and socio-economic backgrounds, age, health and physical characteristics, attitudes, aptitudes, and motivation must be accommodated within the confines of a neighborhood school building. Frequently, many of these variances are further compounded by problems of attrition and migration of students and families.

The Differing Staff

The leadership of a school building is challenged to accommodate staff differences of a personal and professional nature brought about by age, experience, preparation, and past practices. Elements of instructional style and philosophy tend to create differing instructional methods and procedures. The quantity, quality, orientation, and availability of staff resource specialists is another contribution to building level staffing peculiarities. The building leadership style may be progressive, reactionary, sensitive, insensitive, ambitious, stultifying, permissive, restrictive, dynamic, or dull.

The Differing School Program Elements

The instructional schedule is often dominated by building and staff characteristics. Programs of differing structure require supplies and materials of differing quantity, quality, variety, and accessibility. Class size and grade grouping characteristics produce differing program considerations. The variety of furnishings and equipment must be selected to best serve the instructional program. The curriculum design and implementation strategy requires qualities of timeliness, comprehensiveness, flexibility, enrichment, and the satisfaction of district objectives. The accommodation of special student needs is yet another aspect of the required divergence of local school programs.

The Differing School Locales

Each neighborhood is characterized in its progeny. The socio-economic patterns of housing are imposed on neighborhood schools. Community identification with the local school unit leads to community interest, understanding, and support of the local school's efforts. Extended use of school facilities make the buildings particularly valuable to neighborhood interests. Clubs, bands, sports, cultural programs and exhibitions, meetings and matters politic all take a neighborhood flavor.

If all these elements were to be centrally budgeted, a Solomon-like perception would be required in order to promote any semblance of equality, yet these conditions exist in each school district and historically have allegedly been "fairly" treated in terms of resource distribution. Or have they?

School Site Budgeting

School site budgeting offers three unique practices for providing equivalent resource allocations to all the schools (and pupils) of a district:

1. Salaries are adjusted to the district average and dealt with on a building level only in terms of averages.

2. Basic costs, not related to a single building, are maintained in a centrally administered budget.

3. All other available funds are assigned to school buildings on a per capita (though sometimes weighted) basis.

Variations and refinements of these three criterion enable a wide range of local options. Resource allocation decisions are made at the school building level. Substantiation for such a process is found in the report of the President's Commission on School Finance:[7]

> "The whole area of the application of educational resources and investment to effective schooling is extremely complex and clearly cannot be equated directly with

28

input-output analyses of other industries and services. But, to the extent that measures of educational need and educational effectiveness can be developed, they ought to be translated somehow into a system that permits discretion on the part of supervisors, principals, and teachers in their applications. Resources distributed to the schools are often defined in terms of days of substitute teachers' pay or other units of educational measurement. But when a principal wants to send a class of an absent teacher to a zoo or put the class in the auditorium for some special programs, he may find that all he can get for this purpose is the pay allotment for a substitute teacher, when what he needs is a chartered bus or a couple of movies and a projector. The rigidity of such controls of educational practice demonstrates the need for translating alternative resource applications into some freely usable common denominator. One that comes readily to mind, of course, is money, which has a transferability as a resource that surpasses anything any state or district board could possibly devise. In the hands of a principal or teacher, it can provide a variety of educational experience that could not possibly be anticipated by anybody who writes rule books. We urge that this kind of flexibility be made available throughout school systems, districts, and schools, with proper checks and balances. Our research has revealed that many of the presumptions about proper uses of educational resources have not been established to the point where hard and fast rules can be laid out. Children learn in many ways; teachers teach in many ways. Some children learn better from one teacher than another and by one method better than another. Until education becomes an exact science, we ought to encourage as much flexibility as possible."

If decision making is to take place at the school building level, a series of conflicts and competing ideas will occur when educational goals are being developed - much like hard choices in the world outside

29

of the classroom. Choices are often the result of compromise. The process of school site budgeting brings people to a decision making forum. Creative thinking provides an analytical approach to a situation compounded by shifts of authority from a central head-quarters to a local school building group.

It would be difficult to justify school level decisions on any other basis than "what's best for the student". Decisions are being made very close to the students' level of subsistence. Professional rational-ization cannot support instructional decisions based on job security, conditions of employment, past practices or work rules. At the core of decisions regarding staff and materials (and a balance of each) lies the matter of pupil welfare. Only in terms of pupil well-being can there be discussions of class size, paraprofess-ionals, homework, written composition, planning periods, grading, grouping, schedules, libraries, or pupil-staff ratios.

Programs must be priority funded in a series of "go, no go" decisions. Decisions are analyzed in terms of people (staff) and things (instructional materials).

The remainder of this book will sustain the thesis of school site budgeting as an improved process for promoting equality of educational opportunity.

In speaking of equality of educational opportunity as brought about by the Brown vs Board of Education[8] decision, James Farmer wrote:

> "The goal is no longer equal access - equal right to enroll in a school or sit in a class-room. It is now equal results. It is to employ methods and materials and programs capable of closing gaps in educational achievement. And still further, the objective is to raise the educational level of the whole nation, for the attainment of equality on any level below that of excellence is now perceived to be an empty triumph."[9]

1. Serrano vs Priest, California Supreme Court
    938254, L.A. 29820 (1971).

2. Brown vs Board of Education of Topeka, 347
    U.S. 483.

3. John Shannon, "The Role of the State in
    Equalizing Educational Opportunity - An ACIR
    Legislative Proposal", Proceedings of the Tenth
    National Conference on School Finance, (Washington,
    D.C.: National Education Association, 1967),
    pp. 31-36.

4. Ellwood P. Cubberly, School Funds and Their
    Apportionment, (New York: Teachers College
    Columbia University, 1906), p. 17.

5. F. Dee Sanford, "Variations in Costs Among
    Attendance Centers in a Large High School District:
    A Cost Study", Proceedings of the Tenth National
    Conference on School Finance, (Washington, D.C.:
    National Education Association, 1967), pp. 190-92.

6. James B. Conant, Slums and Suburbs, (New York:
    McGraw Hill Book Co., Inc., 1961), p. 145.

7. "Schools, People and Money, The Need for Educa-
    tional Reform", (Washington, D.C.: Government
    Printing Office, 1972), pp. 61-62.

8. Brown vs Board of Education of Topeka, 347,
    U.S. 483.

9. James Farmer, Toward Equal Education Opportunity,
    A Nation of Learners, (Washington, D.C.: U.S.
    Department of Health, Education and Welfare,
    1976), p. 146.

Chapter 3

EQUALIZING ELEMENTS

Does money make a difference? Will more financial
support provide a better educational program? Will less
financial support provide a diminished educational program? In a gross sense there may be little correlation
between levels of educational expenditures and pupil
achievements. The greatest determinants of educational
expenditure levels are the number of certified staff
members employed and their salaries. This approximates
75% of all school expenditures. Books, supplies, and
other instructional materials consume another 3% of educational expenditures. The remaining 22% is for such
operational support items as transportation, cleaning
and maintenance, utilities, secretarial services, and
insurance. It appears that the foremost influence on
instructional programs is the 78% combined for staff
and instructional materials. To equitably distribute
those allocations is the purpose of this book, and hopefully the results will provide improved assignment of
resources to match the needs of each student.

Is it enough to arrange for equivalent instructional input offerings in order to obtain equivalent
learning outcomes? Some research findings bolster the
argument for eliminating carbon copy instructional offerings as a solution to the learning modes of students.

In examining the components of an instructional
program, much research has been devoted to pupil achievement test scores as the measure of discrimination or
validation of findings. The reader should be aware of
the shortcomings of this single measure of performance
which only defines quantifiable outcomes. A complete
educational process includes many other important but
difficult to measure outcomes: attitudes, creative expression, value discrimination, citizenship, curiosity,
moral values, problem solving, organizational skills,
social consciousness, and many latent outcomes.

To advance the argument for school site budgeting,
it is necessary to examine the potential for equalizing
educational opportunities through the assignment of
equivalent resources. It is then necessary to analyze
some elements of instruction in order to understand
their relative influence on educational programs.

Teachers. High salaries do not necessarily produce
the best in teaching practice. It is more likely that
high salaries can provide selective recruitment of the
most able teachers. And, high salaries may incorporate
time commitments to encompass a vital in-service instructional improvement involvement. High salaries
might also indicate a multitude of advanced training
and degree attainment. And, high salaries may indicate
a seasoned and experienced staff of professionals. Conversely, high salaries sometimes indicate a group of
senior staff members with recent little upgrading but
with political clout to support their longevity.

Some research findings have dealt with the factor
of teachers in assessing the quality of educational
programs. Culling through 100 research studies cover-
ing a twenty year period, Heim and Perle[1] found that
83% of the studies concluded that better educated
teachers (higher than average level of teacher education) produced the more impressive student performance.
All of the non-cognitive (attitudes, values, inter-
personal relationships) output studies and 75% of the
cognitive (factual knowledge, conceptual understanding)
output studies attested to this phenomenon.

There was a somewhat lesser relationship between
teacher experience and student performance. In only
57% of the cases, teacher experience was shown to be
related to student performance. A refinement of this
circumstance was evidenced in a Philadelphia study[2]
that found that high achievers do better with more experienced teachers but low achievers evidence a slower
learning growth with more experienced teachers and
seemingly did better with relatively inexperienced
teachers. The study cited the undampened enthusiasm of
new teachers dealing with those who found learning more
difficult. Some studies show that teacher experience
between 3 and 10 years is most helpful as an aid to
pupil achievement.

The Heim and Perle[3] review also noted that the
teacher socio-economic status or verbal ability measures
were significantly related to student performance levels
both cognitive and non-cognitive.

And even with the right mix of teacher preparation,
experience, socio-economic or verbal ability, there is
the matter of teaching method and style to be considered
Differences occur when teachers engage in lectures,

34

discussions, laboratory experiences, guided learning, independent study, simulation, and in the use of print and non-print materials. All such factions need to be analyzed when reviewing equivalent educational offerings for students.

Class Size. All teachers are somewhat affected in their job performance by the number of students for which they are responsible and the groups or blocks in which they are assembled for instructional purposes. Also, the range of student achievements and abilities contained within the instructional block has a direct affect on both the teaching process and the resultant learning.

The issue of class size is not a recent result of collective bargaining privileges as some critics may suggest. The 5th century (BC) Greek historian, Herodotus, described "classes of thirty". More recently, Glass and Smith found that children who gain 1.0 grade equivalents on average per year in a class of 40 would gain 1.3 equivalents in a class of 20, and 1.6 if taught individually. Average pupils, assigned to a class of 20 for kindergarten and the first six grades, would exceed similar pupils in a class of 40 by two years, over the same length of time.[4]

There is not a simple and direct universal relationship between class size and student achievement. However, while the optimum class size has not been identified for all pupils, something has been learned about extreme ranges of class size and how students with differing personal and academic properties respond to smaller class size.

The obvious advantages of small class sizes include more availability for personal contact, peer group instructional pollination, monitoring of individual needs and progress, and smaller scale handling of students' assignments, tests, homework, paper corrections, and supplies and materials acquisitions. Not to be overlooked is the general teacher satisfaction that comes with smaller class sizes. Conversely, larger classes exacerbate these instructional ingredients. But, there is a lack of evidence to substantiate precise levels of benefits emanating from specific class sizes. A review of 50 years of research showed that student achievement increases as class size is reduced, with a large change occuring when classes meet or go below fifteen. Only a small difference in achievement occurs when class size is reduced from twenty-eight to twenty-five.[5]

Many of the potential gains from smaller class sizes are not realized if teachers use the same instructional practices in smaller classes as in large classes. The instruction may be no more individualized despite the easier access to individual students.

Class size is a major determinant of school system budgets. A change of even one or two pupils per class can have a major impact on the overall budget of a school district. Cumulative research of class size phenomena suggest that the methods and quality of instruction in the classroom are considerably more important than the quantity of pupils within the classroom.

Cost: Benefit. The measurement of the educational production function is subject to a vast number of variables. Some studies have measured inputs as a function of quality; number, preparation, and salaries of teachers, time schedules, class size, available facilities and financial appropriations. Other studies have examined output as a function of quality: achievement test results, scholarship awards, acceptances by higher educational institutions, and subsequent success in life. Still others review the instructional process as a measure of quality: curriculum structure, methods of presentation and interplay, tests and reinforcements, enrichment activities, and measures of disciplinary incidents. When further sophistication decrees that cost-benefit analysis takes place, few studies provide unqualified conclusions. Inputs, processes, and benefits are discretely measurable. But their correspondence, factored for time and displacement and the non-school influences on students, is extremely complex. Available tests can at best provide an indication of the monitoring of certain facts. They suffer from an imprecision to measure the breadth of knowledge or depth of understanding that students have gained as a result of their classroom experiences.

Some have attempted cost-benefit and cost-effectiveness studies of instructional enterprise. The search was for a precise model whereby the results of changing various ingredients would produce highly predictable results in the format of a linear relationship.

36

While test results show higher marks in school districts providing higher educational expenditures, the studies have the inherent bias of reflecting wealthier suburban communities comprising the offspring of higher earning and better educated parents. While the results are consistent, conclusions about cost related instructional effectiveness are less reliable.

High expenditure school systems do tend to attract and employ more and better teachers and to support them with plentiful instructional materials and functional facilities. Such school systems have better attendance and have more students stay in school longer. The achievement scores of such students tend to be higher. Higher expenditures for education tend to buy a better educational system, other things being equal. And, it appears that the upper limits of cost-benefit improvements of education have not yet been determined, the point at which additional expenditures would produce little or no further gains.

In a discussion of equivalent educational opportunities, some consideration must be accorded the raw disequal nature of students. It would compound disparity to apply equal learning experiences to students of disequal backgrounds, talents, aspirations, attitudes, conditioning, reading comprehension, verbal ability, or computational skills.

Students of lower socio-economic background tend to show greater gains in school when placed in smaller classes. On a broader scale it was discovered that socio-economic status was a significant variable in almost 88% of recent studies summarized by Heim and Perl.[6] The achievement of culturally and economically poor youngsters is affected by their away from school environment, which frequently does not supplement their intellectual growth and development by promoting sound study habits. There may also be little family influence on motivation, aspiration, or academic stimulation. Sometimes, necessary part-time employment in menial jobs takes time and energy from non-school supplemental learning activities. Still other studies have examined student achievement from the basis of racial differences of pupils. While such studies have found differing results, not clearly isolated from socio-economic factors, the need for variable educational treatment of race (cultural) differences is evident.

The Time Dimension. The utilization of time is another classroom variable to be considered when promoting equitable assignment of resources. Classroom time is spent in several categories: giving instruction, evaluation or monitoring of pupil progress, discipline, giving directions, classroom management, supervision, clerical work, and planning. While some allocations of time are a matter of teaching mode or style, others are products of curriculum make-up, availability of suitable instructional materials, and the needs of learners. Class size may have a direct bearing on the time periods assigned to specific activities. If, as some research suggests, problems of classroom discipline are eased in smaller classes, less time would be taken from instruction.

In The Productive School, J. Allen Thomas provides, "a general principle that the lower one is in the organizational hierarchy, the more his decisions will involve allocating time rather than money".[7] He traces that concept from (1) school district level, to (2) school level, to (3) classroom level, to (4) the student level. Each subsequent level makes fewer monetary decisions but more time-based decisions. Thus, as a resource, time needs to be constructively manipulated for a maximizing effect. Teachers' time is purchased as the highest single cost of operating a school. The manner of planning, scheduling, and interaction intervals with students is most likely to affect the production function of a school. And, because of the differences in learning rates, and the different values associated with some objectives, decisions of time expenditures should be made by the learner. Flexibility is required to permit experimentation and discovery of the best fit with desired production outcomes. Given the sequential nature of learning, the matter of individual pace becomes paramount. Students of similar ability can master equivalent bodies of knowledge, but not at the same rate.

One study of California primary school teachers showed that approximately 20% of their morning class time was devoted to instruction, defined as "acts of imparting skills and knowledge". A summary of their use of time showed percentages of:

Instruction	20.2%
Planning for instruction	10.9%
Evaluation of instruction	22.4%

Classroom management	18.4%
Supervision	8.2%
Clerical	2.8%
Preparation of facilities	1.3%
Administration	2.8%
Preparation of materials	5.1%
Non-teaching	7.9%

The study indicated that these time allocations were greatly altered when the teachers were provided with the services of an instructional aide.[8]

Fiscal Equity. School site budgeting is designed to provide a fair share of financial resources for the customized betterment of each student. Given such funding, school principals and teachers can best channel the money to the areas of greatest need or those having potential to do the greatest good. But, such decisions are highly localized and non-standardized. It is important that funding allocations filter down at least to the classroom level. Discretionary expenditures should be available to meet the varying needs of each student. Some will most benefit from a basic text, while others will gain from having supplemental texts, a different text, supportive reference materials, manipulative paraphernalia, mock-ups and models, multisensory (audio-visual) presentations, guest instructors, charts and graphic materials, puzzles and games, self-paced programmed materials, teacher made materials, drill materials, or even field trips to museums, factories, or places of historic, geographic, or social significance. By having financial resources available for use, unencumbered, frequent and well timed decisions can be made to accommodate the learning style or peculiar requirements of each student. In a dynamic learning environment of multi-materials, a lot of cross-pollination and fertilization occurs between students. Given the diversity of materials, the normal traits of inquisitiveness, peer group envy, imitation, mimicry, and intellectual competition all work to produce a healthful exploratory experience. Students are in a very desirable environment of revalation and discovery through such a variety of heady occurrences.

Such diversity need not entail large financial costs. Low cost materials from newspapers, periodicals, corporate advertising publications, or teacher made substances may be a better trade-off to a universal textbook focused on the middle range of the subject and designed for a normative level of reading comprehension. That just may not be good enough for the normally curved one-third of a class of pupils that do not cluster about the middle.

Researchers discriminate between the cost-benefit and the cost-effectiveness of resource assignments. Cost-benefit analysis tends to determine the input-output ratio without particularly focusing on, or caring about, the intermediate process that takes place. From a carload of raw materials, the manufacturer has produced a quantity of finished product. The difference between the present value of benefits and the present value of costs is the internal rate of return. To improve that ratio, the manufacturer would have to turn to a cost-effectiveness analysis.

Effectiveness. In the quest for equity and equality of instructional offerings, practitioners should understand the relationship between effectiveness and efficiency. In striving for efficiency, there can be a sacrificing of effectiveness. It is possible to have an efficient public education system (one with low unit costs) that is not effective, just as it is possible to have an effective system that is not efficient.

In education the cost is defined as the resources utilized, and the benefits as the learning experiences that students gather. The effectiveness measure would examine the process variables to improve the intended rate of return. Precluding an exercise in semantics, the thrust of school site budgeting is to improve the benefits which the student acquires by re-affirming the notion of individuality and strengthening the elements of learning.

Defining Equity. School site budgeting purports to provide equivalent educational opportunities for all students. This does not mean that each student should be rendered precisely the same instructional experiences. The issue must be expanded to consideration of equity, a word having connotations of fairness and justice; something which supplements and deals with those things which are not covered by ordinary procedures or practices. Schools must make accommodation of pupil differences. Special education programs for gifted, atypical, or handicapped students are an illustration of the provision of different treatment of different needs: an equitable solution. On a slightly

lesser scale, the cultivation of vital opportunities
for the divergent needs of each regular classroom pupil
is an indication of providing equivalent (but different)
educational opportunities. If an equal solution appears
to be a good response, it is only by chance. Ordinarily
an equal dispensing of an instructional offering results
in being the exact solution for very few constituents.
Such push-button solutions may be administratively con-
vient but are apt to be pedagogically indefensible, so
long as students are not cloned.

1. John Heim and Lewis Perl, "The Educational Produc-
    tion Function: Implications for Educational Man-
    power Policy", (Ithica, N.Y.: New York State School
    of Industrial and Labor Relations, Cornell Univer-
    sity, 1974), p. 11.

2. Anita A. Summers and Barbara L. Wolfe, "Which School
    Resources Help Learning? Efficiency and Equity in
    Philadelphia Public Schools", Business Review,
    (Philadelphia: Federal Reserve Bank of Philadelphia,
    February, 1975), p. 13.

3. John Heim and Lewis Perl, op. cit., p. 12.

4. General D. Haertel, Diane Schiller, and Herbert J.
    Walberg, "The Quiet Revolution in Educational
    Research", Phi Delta Kappan, Vol. 61, no. 3, 1979,
    p. 180.

5. Leonard S. Cahen and Nikola N. Filby, "The Class
    Size/Achievement Issue", Phi Delta Kappan, Vol. 60,
    No. 7, 1979, p. 492.

6. John Heim and Lewis Perl, op. cit., p. 10.

7. J. Allen Thomas, "The Productive School", (New York:
    John Wiley and Sons, Inc., 1971) p. 41.

8. Diana B. Hiatt, "Time Allocation in the Classroom:
    Is Instruction Being Shortchanged?", Phi Delta
    Kappan, Vol. 61, No. 4, 1979, p.p. 289-90.

Chapter 4

THE SCHOOL SITE BUDGETING PROCESS

School site budgeting is a process for providing the full capability for local schools to plan their future operations in a manner to best serve the instructional needs of their students. The process has five basic parts:

1. The establishment of an overall district budget target.

2. The establishment of basic (non school site) costs.

3. The assignment of all remaining funds to individual schools on a per capita basis.

4. The development of individual school expenditure plans.

5. The assembly of individual school expenditure plans into a comprehensive district budget in accordance with #1.

George Santayana observed that the great difficulty in education is to get experience out of ideas. An up-front commitment to experience school site budgeting would include awareness of several propositions.

Individuality. Each learner is important at all times and should receive the exact instruction required and equal access to educational opportunity. While some batch processing training, drill, or reinforcement of experiences can be efficiently accomplished, the higher purpose of schools is to pinpoint the exact learning needs of each student. There must be building level acquaintanceship with each student in order to diagnose and prescribe suitable instructional responses. These diagnoses will vary among students, grade levels, and school buildings. Even where similar needs are observed in students in different school buildings, the availability of resources and instructional methodology might indicate differing instructional procedures. The important element is the making of building level decisions for the design of each student's educational endeavors; one of a kind decisions. When beginning the process of school site budgeting, the instructional targets must first be agreed upon.

System-wide goals. Building leaders have the freedom to plan and execute instructional programs for each student. To do so implies an ability to marshal and direct resources as required. But first, there must be a pre-ordained direction, an educational goal. Such goals become a magnetic force for all students of the school district. Students must achieve a common set of specific objectives in order to meet the higher echelon system-wide goals. Educational objectives are expressed according to the subject, program, function, or academic discipline. The objectives should be measurable, observable, or assessable in some agreed manner. It should be possible to certify when the common objectives have been fulfilled by each student. Students will require different materials and lessons as they strive for the learning objectives. Some students will require a different block of time or some tutorial assistance, while others will need a variety of stimuli and/or a logical sequential or juxtaposed presentation of information. Each learning style must be accommodated. Since students seldom spend their entire schooling career in a single building, the matter of progressive migration into secondary school buildings requires student achievement of a common set of objectives at each preceding level of instruction.

Best use of funds. The school site budgeting process has dollar stretching capabilities. When financial allocations are dissected at the building level, expenditures are more closely reviewed. Each expenditure is planned on a net basis to achieve a very specific result. Funding is dealt with in smaller, better understood, and more manageable parcels. There is less cause for potentially wasteful assignment of funds to unspecified contingency accounts. Such accounts often produce crash expenditures rather than planned purchases. They lead to charges of inflated or padded budgeting which is detrimental to the creation of public confidence in the financial planning for school operations. School site budgeting creates added accounting units which have the advantage of displaying financial matters in greater detail. Each school becomes a cost center. Greater understanding of school fiscal needs, uses, and audits are achieved. Funding can be traced to a program, a grade level, a class, or even to an individual pupil if desired. Such micro-budgeting has long been practiced by commercial and industrial firms in the private sector. The greatest financial advantage of school site budgeting is the expectation that money allocations will provide the correct ingredients to link each pupil's instructional needs to the best available resources. The process might not produce a reduction in educational expenditures, but there should be a high correlation between expenditures and needs. Educational issues are described in a financial dimension when schools pinpoint the unit costs of their efforts. Such a display should lead to improved (more informed) decision making.

Freedom to choose. There is no pattern to follow when initially determining how allocated funds can best be engaged to serve a school's needs. Some kind of a priority order must be developed. Sensible administrators will involve staff members, parents, community leaders and upper grade level students when picking the options that seem most worthy of fund assignment. Just as the bridge of a ship is a lonely command post, the administrator of a school is sometimes in a position often isolated from the sensitivities of the publics to be served. School site budgeting fosters participatory decision making when no pre-ordained constraints are present.

Typically there are many alternatives available when schools gear up to meet specific instructional objectives. A very basic decision is to determine which objectives currently require greater effort for fulfillment. Often, test results will tell where shortcomings occur. When the problems are identified, the blend of strategic responses can vary by such components as staff assignments and allocations, materials provided, time assignments, external enrichments, integrated or segregated curriculum presentations, homework, tutoring, customized reinforcement, or further diagnostic testing. The important thing is to observe that schools have the choices available to them and they need only exercise them. As earlier mentioned, there are very few decisions that are reserved for a central administrative unit. Such matters are generally restricted to non-instructional housekeeping matters and such items as wages, accounting, legislated mandates, business and other support services. All other decisions are made at the building level: number and type of staff, materials and services to be purchased, instructional strategies to be employed, and decisions of class size, student grouping, and monitoring and assessment of instructional progress. There's a timeliness and responsiveness in the school site budgeting process that

permits and encourages such choices. This should result
in the right amount of instructional weaponry being
brought to bear on tactically diagnosed instructional
necessities. School systems do not possess the communications capabilities to centrally warehouse instructional resources and quickly and efficiently convey them to
the areas where and when instruction is taking place.

With local freedom of choice, progress can be
likened to John Dewey's comment regarding intellectual
discovery: "Every great advance in science has issued
from a new audacity of imagination."

Pinpoint responsibility. This feature of the
school site budgeting process provides a swift and sure
response to adjust classroom situations as necessary.
The local building administrator is firmly in control
of the instructional process as carried out throughout
the building. There can be no alibi for non-awareness.
The building leaders' involvement with all aspects of
the school program could be likened to the maxim of a
boxing ring where one fighter said, "He can run, but
he can't hide." The building leader may often need the
responses of a boxer in knowing when to bob, weave,
feint, parry, thrust, jab, counter punch, and move
forward to attack the range of instructional decisions
required.

The subrogation of responsibility to a school
level does not in itself assure complete fulfillment
of educational objectives. It does, however, provide
a means for isolating the components for review. The
troublesome elements may transcend the arsenal of the
building leader's response. In such cases, assistance
from a central authority may be required. Such assistance may include consultation, the retention of expert diagnosticians, supplemental financial appropriations, schedule modifications, personnel assignments
and transfers, or the transfer of students to a more
suitable school environment. Even with all such higher
level responses, the responsibility for initiating such
actions must come from the local building leader. For
most situations, the local school administrators provide
daily decisions to routine instructional problems. And
like the boxer mentioned above, the building leader
mostly wins, occasionally loses, and often gets a split
decision. Most often in dealing with divergent and competing ideas, a split decision is the right choice to
seek. To understand how the best use of available funds

is made when school unit administrators make spending decisions, let's move to examining the mechanics of school site budgeting.

Determination of funding. Since school site budgeting requires a rationalized assignment of money to each school, it would follow that the sum to be distributed must be arrived at as a part of a larger budgetary sphere.

Education, in principle, enjoys a hallowed reputation and is regularly funded as an element of government. Most states have created legislation promoting specific facets of education and have correspondingly enacted legislation to provide for funding of the required activities. Being a fluid social process, education seldom stands still and remains stifled or bounded by special purpose legislation. As instructional method and content are constantly revised, their funding needs are equally changing. Since at any given time 20% of the population consists of students in a school environment, the political process is ready to accept responsibility for adequate school funding. It is politically difficult to determine what a suitable financial authorization for educational purposes should be. Something more than 50% of local governmental costs are apt to be set aside for schools.

In the past, varying formulas have sought to determine education's share of tax dollars. But all such formulas have been insensitive to changes in the volume, scope, and comprehensiveness of what is taught. Such factors as a reduction in grade retentions, increased holding power for potential drop-outs, and a better diagnosis of special pupils' learning disabilities have all worked to out-pace rigid expenditure assignment formulae.

Some educational improvements have resulted from local level research activities. As in any form of research, some failures often precede successes. When such educational research failures are viewed in isolation, the uninitiated on-lookers might conclude that the financial support of some such activities is wasteful. While such costs cannot be ignored, they should not restrict growth and development in such human fulfillment fields as education or medicine. The raw cost of a surgical procedure or particular type of instruction should not be the determinant of its worth or value.

47

How then can the right amount of tax receipts be determined in order to provide a reasonable and adequate educational program? Political leaders need to be aided in their search for an answer to that question. Discussions are entered into early in the budget preparation cycle. The intent is to tentatively set educational allocations in advance of firing a barrage of certified "needs". Whenever the financial dimensions of educational needs exceed a reasonable share of currently levied revenues, legislative leaders are put in a bargaining role. In this mode they may adhere to reason, but often revert to emotions as a basis for analysis. The process produces a gap which is hard to bridge through nominal compromise.

There is a common denominator: the amount that is currently assigned to schools. Community political leaders realize that the memory of the electorate spans about five minutes. Decisions at the polls tend to be based on current happenings and on promises of future services or behavior. The amount set aside for schools last year (the current budget limit) becomes history. Unless special circumstances occur, leaving indelible impressions, the element of time will have defused the pro and con positions regarding the degree of funding provided for schools some 12 to 18 months ago. If the schools appear to be operated on an even keel without evidence of exaggeration, redundancy, or waste, and there are no outcrys from being deprived or hampered by shortages, hindsight might show that the current allocation for schools is about right.

An analogy could be made by showing a buyer (taxpayer) as one who consistently wants to get the item as cheaply as possible. Yet, the seller (the school board) consistently wants to get the highest amount possible - the age old merchandising syndrome. And, since the buyer has most of the options, the seller cannot afford to overstate the case! When that occurs, the seller's credibility is vacated and the school board resembles the shepherd who cried "wolf!". Consumers of education can often buy the service from alternate (private school) sources - leading to an erosion of support by being (doubly) taxed for public schools. One superintendent of schools once said, "We may be the only public school system in Town but we'd better not act that way."

<u>Can school site budgeting be legalized</u>? A few
legal obstacles may exist when school site budgeting is
proposed. Such obstacles generally would not become
barriers. Heretofore states have dealt with education
only on a school district basis. A complete re-thinking
is required to cope with schools on a building basis.
Extant funding legislation may contain requirements
which are too gross for building level applicability.
A sample statute says, "All educational allocations
shall be approved by a majority vote of the Board of
Education." When a school site decision requires a
substitution of one textbook for another, for the use
of a few children, it would be an obstacle to first
return to the Board of Education for a permissive fund
transfer. Such obstacles can be overcome through
reasoning, interpretation, and the good-will efforts
of parties involved.

School site budgeting is a planning device - a way
of getting schools to simulate responses to their genuine and self-perceived needs! It need not conflict
with any known statute since it may (1) precede mandated
formal budgetary preparation regimens, (2) deal in
assumptions rather than enactments, and (3) be sufficiently pliable to eventually be transformed into any
statutory format. In the worst case, a school district
would maintain a dual set of financial accounts: one as
mandated, and one as locally desired for improved
planning and control purposes (school site budgeting).
Usually one process will suffice, since with data processing capabilities reassembly of data to other formats
is an easy task.

<u>The elements of popular opinion</u>. Much of the
attractiveness of the school site budgeting concept is
the public acceptance of its basic straight forward
nature. With a minimum of ceremony, it plunges schools
and school constituents into a process of actively
planning for the healthful function of the neighborhood school. And as a bonus, the local budget planners
are assured that their school is receiving the same
financial support as all other schools of the district
since appropriations are based solely on the number and
nature of students assigned to or expected to enroll at
the school. Public confidence is further generated by
the openness of having school expenditure decisions
arrived at in a fish bowl environment. No funds are
withheld from the budget setting sessions nor are any
gross exaggerations acceptable concerning funding needs.

Whatever funds are available, their future use is an openly debated issue. People start to realize the difficult nature of picking from within a series of suggestions or requests or demands those needs which are to be satisfied. It's a form of government by immersion. While few citizens have cause to be well versed in an entire school system budget, many residents would relate to the closest neighborhood school. Such persons are to be invited to actively plan for their school's needs. A taxpayer identity problem is on the way to resolution or remediation. When a single system-wide budget is eventually formulated (from all the individual school budgets) legislative reviewers sit up and take notice upon learning that thousands of people have helped plan the budgets of the schools. Politicians respect numbers, even to putting aside their own feelings concerning the amount of money to be made available for school purposes.

By determining the costs of education in advance of the item expenditure decision, an opportunity is provided for parents, staff, and other school oriented personages to genuinely share in making such decisions. The determination of how the money is to be used can be better made before it becomes (even tentatively) earmarked as in conventional budgeting. Formerly, citizen participation was mostly present after the school budget had been formulated and was being presented in public to a legislative funding authority - too late for substantial changes. Often, such participation was of a negative orientation by persons uninvolved or uninformed of the basis for expenditure decisions. School site budgeting provides meaningful up-front involvement in planning expenditures and subsequent program decisions.

So, conceptually it can be shown that a school site budgeting process will enhance the need for large numbers of persons becoming active in politics (albeit for schools). It can also be demonstrated that legal barriers would not work to prevent most simulation activities designed to explore the worth of a school site budgeting process. Above all, it connotes a thrust for each school and child having an equal opportunity to receive the best education that the school district can provide.

Estimating major cost elements. In attempting

to set the overall ceiling for educational expenditures, an analysis is required of the major expense items to be incorporated. These include personnel costs, materials costs, newly mandated elements, program changes, and any variance in the size of the pupil population.

Planning for Personnel Costs. Personnel costs may make up more than 80% of a school district operating budget. It is the pivotal issue affecting school costs. There are three parts to personnel cost determinations: wage scales, number of persons employed, and fringe benefits.

Wage scales are the most significant determiner of educational costs. They need to be typical of a locale and they must be readily adjustable. Looking ahead for one or more years is easily achieved if a multi-year wage agreement is in effect. It's a matter of projecting the change in wage scales as a per cent. The same percentage applied to the salary portion of the budget will provide the major ingredient of a new budget target.

	New Contract	Increase Due To Salaries
Current Budget $16,000,000 100%		
Certified Salaries $11,600,000 73%	6.0% ($696,000)	
Classified Salaries $ 1,900,000 12%	5.5% ($104,500)	
Other Costs $ 2,500,000 15%		
		5.0% ($800,500)

To implement new wage rates while maintaining the present staff would show a gross increase of 5% in the overall budget. If new wage contracts were not settled at budget planning time, an assumed settlement goal can be inserted into the planning process exactly as above. These data should include total wage costs resulting from advancement of employees within the scales (incremental) and gross adjustments to the wage scales.

The second element of personnel cost planning is the number of persons to be employed. If a significant number are to be added or deleted, their total wage impact may be applied to the percentage increase proposed for the next planning cycle. If the change is to take place sometime within the fiscal period, only the proportionate share of the change should be included.

The third element of planning for personnel costs is the amount of money required to provide employee benefits. In some cases employee benefits may be equal to 40% of wages when all insurance, leave, holiday, retirement and perquisites are tallied. These are listed third since their cost is dependent upon the number of persons employed and their salary levels. When the total benefit cost is known, it too is applied to the amount sought to fund schools for the next budgetary period.

While these elements of personnel costs may be calculated separately (wage scales, number of employees, benefits), there is an undeniable relationship between and among the three. Often, higher wages bring about increased productivity and fewer workers. Higher wages may cause a tightening of work rules thereby reducing the labor force. Conversely, lower wage scales may lead to featherbedding and inflation of the required number of employees. The largest determinant of the number of positions to be funded is that of pupil/staff ratio. If that element is to be changed in any way, particularly with assumptions concerning class size, the upcoming budget target should accommodate and reflect that circumstance. The issue of employee benefits is usually considered only after wages and staffing decisions are made. As benefit costs mount, it is likely that they will soon be resolved up-front, as part of a wage consideration.

Summing up, personnel costs are the largest determinant of the educational expenditure level and as such should be the first decision element for establishing a reasonable target for educational expenditures. Such costs may be calculated on the basis of multi-year labor agreements or may be estimated by simulating realistic goals for future wage settlements.

Mandated Expenditure Requirements. After plotting the impact of personnel costs, an examination of school

program changes might further indicate the cosmos of
future cost estimates. With increased equalization
concerns being foisted at the state level, local schools
are often caught up in trying to meet new (unfunded)
mandates. As state-wide instructional thrusts emerge
with such concepts as accommodation of handicapped
students, career preparation, and competency assessment efforts, local schools need to isolate and calculate the costs of such changes and expose their
impact on future expenditure targets. Yet other costly
program changes could be attributed to collectively
bargained agreements, accreditation requirements, or
programs having a long term sequential phase in.

Major cost elements may also be mandated by external forces such as inflationary spiralling of the
costs for goods and services, major repairs to facilities, upkeep of equipment, utility rate variations,
experience rated insurance policies, compliance with
state or local governmental regulations, and items of
health and safety. All such phenomena have implied
cost changes, generally on an additive basis. By
committing them to tabular summarization, their combined effort can be applied to the development of a
target for educational support funding.

Population Changes Affecting Future Costs. The
current general decline in educational enrollments
provides a challenge of matching pupil reductions with
cost reductions. Simply stated, there is no mesh between the two entities. The enrollment decline was
caused by a change in the birth rate. The lowered
number of live births seeps into schools on a gradual
basis starting with kindergarten enrollments. Therefore, the lowered pupil population data culls out students at the lowest (and least expensive) grades. The
most expensive secondary school student programs, by
remaining intact, consume a larger share of (lesser)
educational appropriations. And, for similar reasons,
staff reductions first become available at the primary
grades. Even then, most reduction-in-force clauses in
labor agreements specify reverse seniority as the basis
for terminating employees. This means that the last
persons hired, being less experienced and compensated
at the lowest rates, are the persons to be released as
a result of declining enrollments. In so doing, the
higher paid (experienced) teachers tend to skew the wage
average upwards. If the same pupil-teacher ratios are
maintained, except with a greater proportion of higher

paid teachers, the per pupil costs will <u>increase</u> in a period of declining enrollment!

Similarly, a declining pupil population will not permit lowered maintenance, operation, or fixed costs unless the decline is sufficient in one locale to permit the closing of a school building. Until that occurs, per pupil costs will increase as fewer students are served by non-changing fixed costs. If fixed costs are affected by a general economic inflationary trend, the impact on per pupil costs is even greater

Some costs are directly related to the number of students. A sampling of such costs would include supplies, textbooks, and materials dispensed or consumed on a per capita basis.

Many costs are mostly unaffected by a modest reduction in pupil enrollments: regular transportation and field trips, club activities, administrative and supervisory expenses, cost for heat, light, power, and telephones, cleaning supplies, maintenance of buildings and grounds, capital outlay items, and similar costs not related to individual consumption.

When pupil population reductions are sufficient to close parts of, or entire school buildings, many of the costs associated with plant operation can be applied as expenditure reductions.

When pupil populations are increasing, the opposite of these phenomena occur. Newly hired recent college graduates tend to skew the per pupil costs downward. By scattering a few students among several grades, class sizes creep upwards at a cost saving pace. Unless and until additional administrative, maintenance, or operational fixed costs are needed, the cost per pupil tends to diminish. But, at some point, plant expansions must occur and facility development catches up with student population demands.

whichever direction student population is moving towards, the changes must be factored into estimates of major cost elements for subsequent educational budget setting.

<u>School Program Requirements</u>. It may not be enough to set a school appropriation only by those elements of

personnel costs, program mandates, and population changes. Such responses will only maintain an existing level of service. Should school activities continue to develop and grow? Like swimming against the tide, one must exert a lot of energy just to maintain a position. To make progress, extra effort is required. School site budgeting, as a concept, tends to stifle progressive expansion by putting an early limit on available funding (and expenditures). To counteract that restrictive tendency, a school district might set aside a sum of money for growth and development. The money could be earmarked or reserved for pre-determined activities, could be assigned to schools on a per capita basis as a supplement to their normal funds, could be retained at central headquarters for future disbursement, could be awarded to schools on a competitive basis, or could be funnelled to meet a particular need. If such a growth fund is to be established, its effect on the budget target estimate should be considered when all such data are being accumulated.

Other Funding Sources. Categorical grants which do not supplant or displace local efforts should be excluded from the budget target for major planning purposes. Their presence or absence would only have an additive effect on the school or program they propose to alter. The schools would still require a normal compliment of funds for on-going programs. An example of this type of grant would be a grant to a high school which would provide a specialized after school program of vocational education. Such funding is not transferrable or assignable to any other purpose and would not relieve the school of any normal funding obligations.

Non-categorical grants, or grants which may add to or displace funds that would otherwise be provided from a school's allocation, need to be totalled into the budget target figure in order that their benefits may be shared among the entire pupil population. An example would be any of the state or federal employee training or development grants. If unrestricted, some schools could supplant or supplement their regular staffing costs with grant trainees and bring about an unequal application of school funding. Each grant program should be measured by the yardstick of the displacement of local (school building) funding effort.

A distinction is to be made between commonly available funds (accessible to all schools) and earmarked funds which are restricted to only some schools or programs. The common funds should be incorporated into the estimate of the overall budget target and subsequently re-applied equally to all schools.

Level of Support Desired by Schools. Each school has a separate personality caused by the make-up of the staff and students. Administrative style influences the manner in which schools perform. Schools differ in their views of curriculum, school finance, political isms, contemporaneity, methodology, control, and planning efforts. Sister schools will develop different responses to each of these entities. Perceptive administrators charged with helping to formulate the single budget target must gather such information from the schools and process it into a rational position, particularly for those things that a majority of the separate schools independently proffer, whether the items be additive or subtractive.

Level of Support Desired by Community. In some school district as few as 30% of the adults are parents or guardians of pupils enrolled in schools of the community. School leaders must evaluate that limited power base when seeking public support for improved school offerings. Yet, communities often have significant motivation for providing quality schools. Such reasons would include sustenance of property values, community pride, tradition, intellectual enlightenment, and empathy for future generations.

Conversely, there are community members who would seek to repress the schools for reasons of economy, dissatisfaction with school operations, their personal schooling experiences, reactionary viewpoints, or disinterest.

Since each type of person will sway tentatively established school support levels, successful school administrators must encourage the combination of such divergent views in order to establish an acceptable compromised school budget target. General George C. Marshall once observed, "Democracy is the most demanding of all forms of government in terms of the energy, imagination, and public spirit required of the individual".

56

Level of Support Affected by Local Circumstances.
There are times when communities seek a change in the
image or reality of local school operations. Such
changes may be triggered by changes in leadership personalities, shifts of political power, correction of
previous excesses, changes brought about by commercial,
industrial, or residential development, or even road
building or transportation development. Such factors,
if properly interpreted, can affect school spending
targets.

Setting the Overall Financial Target. Elected and
appointed school officials unite in presenting a well
planned proposal for next year's school funding. The
proposal is based on (1) expected pupil population
changes, (2) personnel requests, (3) changes in the
market costs for goods and services, (4) mandated
changes, (5) program improvement efforts, (6) parent
and community desires, (7) special local circumstances,
and (8) labor expectations. All of these elements are
combined and their amalgamated impact is calculated as a
percentage change from the current expenditure level.

If, for example, the gross change recommendation
appears to be a net increase of 7%, that amount would
be tentatively agreed upon as a reasonable target for
next year's school budget limit. The community political leaders should be aware of such a target, and their
suggestions should be sought at the time the gross estimate is being devised. If a formalized legislative
process is yet required at some future time for the
final establishment of a school budget, the planning
process may yet proceed, but on a tentative (simulated)
basis. The agreed target needs to be generally accepted
in order that future bargaining not commence from a
vulnerably slim base. No party to the agreement should
knowingly deflate or kite the figure while hoping for
a later revision. There must be a sincere attempt to
fabricate a school district budget that would approximate the agreed 107% (limit) of current costs.

School site budgeting as a process is sufficiently
flexible to permit formulation of several levels of
expenditure as a planning venture. While some duplicity
and overlapping of planning efforts is entailed, budgets
can be planned to maintain the current funding level-
zero growth, funding at a minimal growth level, or
funding at a desirable growth level. Under those cir-
stances a ranking of needs might show progressive

budgets of 100% of current costs, 107% as minimal responsible growth, and 109% as desirable program growth. Or, in the case of diminishing enrollments the targets might be 100% of current costs, 97% as a moderately phased reduction, or 93% as a minimum expenditure level consistent with minimal program functions. The projected budget target becomes a complicated, critical, timely, and far-reaching decision. It can strangulate, sustain, or stimulate the upcoming programs in the schools.

Designation of Non-site Costs

Some centralized school district costs are not readily assignable to school sites. Such costs are accommodated first, before school site allocations are determined. After estimated basic costs are removed from the appropriation target, all remaining monies are divided among the schools in an equalized manner.

Non-site costs should be restricted to as few thing as possible. Non-site costs should include those things of a non-instructional nature having system-wide application, those things which contribute to school district objectives, items which are not easily pre-assigned to single buildings, things which can be more economically managed to create large volume savings, and school support activities that are variable and randomly related to individual schools. Some examples of each category of basic costs would show:

- Non-Instructional System-wide Costs: central administrative costs, business services, attendance services, dues, fees and memberships, printing, personnel services, staff development, unassigned substitute employees.

- Costs Contributing to School District Objectives: supervisory costs, volunteer program, continuing education, tuition payments, testing expenses, research costs.

- Costs Not Easily Assigned to Single Buildings: data processing, wage reserves, intensive special education classes, facilities rentals.

- Large Volume Efficiency Economies: bulk supplies, cleaning materials, laundry services, food service supplements.

- Randomly Related Support Activities: transportation, maintenace of plant; repairs to equipment, replacement of equipment, snow removal, grounds care.

In determining which items are to be set aside in the basic cost section of the budget planning process, the following questions need to be addressed:

1. Can a local building control the expenditure or is it affected by sources remote from a single school building? (transportation).

2. Is it highly predictable, or subject to chance fluctuation? (maintenance and repairs).

3. Are there cost saving advantages to maintain central control of the object? (paper products).

4. Should a building be burdened with a cost that has little if any bearing on the building's instructional profile? (telephone costs).

5. Should an item be centrally held in escrow for later assignment to a school? (wage reserve).

6. Would accounting costs exceed the net value of the service or item? (data processing).

If an item of expenditure can be classified in any of these categories it should be examined as a potential non-site cost and budgeted within the basic cost category.

When initially adopting the school site budgeting concept it would be advisable to carefully examine the assignment of costs to the basic (central) budget. Aside from the conceptual classification, there is a need for long term comparability of costs. Entries should not vacillate from year to year if meaningful comparisons or trend audits are to be made.

There is a convenience in using the basic cost budget section to accommodate transient, developmental, or pilot programs. Often, such activities have extraordinary start-up expenses that could be best borne by a centralized research support allocation. After new programs become operational they should be made available to the schools and their total cost returned to the school allocation pool.

Central Administration. For successful school site budgeting to occur, it is necessary to provide strong central planning and leadership. If the grand scheme is to be a cohesive whole, it must be carefully constructed, closely monitored, sensitively adjusted, and continuously evaluated. These actions become goals of the system-wide central administrative structure. The substantiation of their purpose requires adequate funding within the basic budget cost section. School critics may allude to the central administrative costs as an overhead burden to the school costs. It is true that funds not expended centrally would be available for the schools' budget pool. This requires the formulation of an efficient central administrative support program clearly designed to service the schools through a set of specific performance goals. Such goals would include: getting resources for schools, logistical support, quality control, and a policy making leadership function. When the central administrative costs are being planned within the basic cost budget, the separate school leaders should have an opportunity to review the proposals and to make suggestions concerning the level of services obtained or desired. It again is a process of getting consensus through participation.

Reserve Accounts. The basic cost section of the budget is a useful repository for funds to be assigned to schools at a future date. One such sum might be held as a wage and benefit reserve. Often, employee contract discussions have not been concluded at budget planning time. In order to be able to fund an eventual settlement, a reserve account is required. The sum might approximate what the final agreement is expected to be or the sum may be a deflated figure, designed as a bargaining tactic. It may be possible to combine estimates for settlement with several employee groups, thereby camouflaging each groups' anticipated share. If there is but a single sum for a lone bargaining unit, it may be split for purposes of concealment. Some share of the sum might be lumped into an employee fringe benefits account for later retrieval. This prevents employee groups from commencing collective bargaining with full knowledge of management's available resources, causing then to push for improvement beyond the advertised "given" limit.

Monies may be reserved in the basic cost budget segment for indeterminate contingent purposes. A sum might be set aside for the emergency needs of school buildings. Such needs would be caused by a rapid infusion of additional students, accidental uninsured losses, any oversights in planning, or crises which unfold during the budget operational period.

All such reserve accounts should be openly administered and guarded against charges of inflating or padding the budget. They should be used solely for the intended purpose, or if necessary, visibly transferred to a purpose having higher priority.

Common Costs. Some cost items are essential to the functioning of a school system yet are not clearly assignable to school buildings nor to central administrative costs. Such common costs belong within the basic cost section of the budget. Examples include: mileage allowances for specialists traveling between schools, large volume supply purchases which are centrally warehoused and dispensed as needed, accounts used to accommodate the salary differences brought about by attrition (the turn-over gain or loss of experienced or non-experienced personnel), and widely dispersed short term special grant programs. Most of such costs could be accounted for by assignment to a school building, but the added accounting costs would most likely exceed the value of the goods or services rendered.

Grouping of Basic (Non-site) Costs. For ease of future convertability, basic costs should be grouped in the format of their ultimate presentation to the legislative authority. Whether the classification is by function, object, program, or expenditure accounts (circa 1966), a consistency of classification will most easily accommodate their transposition to the locally acceptable funding format. When the uniform system has been determined, the elements may be assembled in a grade level array if desirable for further cost planning. The prime reasons for items being assigned to the basic cost section of the budget is their non-tracibility to single schools. However, many such costs would be assigned to grade level groupings such as pre-school, primary, intermediate, elementary, middle, secondary, and post high if cost assignment purposes would be better served.

61

A final reminder: the basic cost section of the budget should contain only those costs which cannot reasonably by assignable to or controlled at a school site. The number of such items requires a continuous review and testing for validity.

Determining School Allocations

After establishing the total budget target and subtracting the required amount to support basic non-site costs, all remaining funds are divided among the individual school buildings on an equitable per capita basis.

The first factor in establishing an equitable basis for allocation is the size of the pupil population to be served; the schools' enrollment. Next, the gross enrollment data must be adjusted to compensate for the varying costs of some grade levels. If kindergarten pupils only attend half day sessions, they should count for only half of a pupil expenditure unit.

Secondary school pupils require a higher expenditure allocation than elementary school pupils. Depending on which costs are assignable to campus activities, the weighting for secondary school pupils may vary between 10% and 35% of more. Secondary school weightings may be arrived at either by plotting expenditures for the past few years and averaging their relationship to elementary school costs or may be arrived at by simulating a model secondary school expenditure pattern. To do so would entail creating assumptions of class sizes and school schedules, staff costs, materials costs, extra-curricular activity costs, supplies, and specialized facilities and paraphernalia. Some national studies limit the range of secondary school costs at 1.2 to 1.3 times elementary school costs. The added costs may be attributed to smaller pupil/staff ratios, flexible scheduling and electives, customized advanced courses, and costly equipment and instructional materials. One user of school site budgeting, Fairfield, Connecticut, used a factor of 1.25 for assigning pupil expenditure units to secondary schools. The index number might also vary according to the grade levels of secondary schools. A different index might be utilized for junior high schools, middle schools, or extended elementary schools. A review of previous expenditures by grade level would provide an initial index for budget planning purposes.

62

At the beginning of a school site budgeting cycle, the estimated enrollment for each school is provided by a central administrative agency or may be jointly developed with neighborhood school input. If a reasonably stabilized pupil population is anticipated, enrollments may be based on the average enrollment occurring at mid-point of a school year. If there are extenuating circumstances that cause a bulge in enrollment at any given time of the year, that peak level might be the most reasonable enrollment assumption for budget planning purposes. Since dollar amounts are to be directly affixed to enrollment projections, it is vital that care and accuracy be the rules of prognostication.

Special Circumstances. At a building level, more than 90% of expenditures will be made for staff salaries. Therefore, anything which affects the routine pupil/staff relationship should be factored into calculations to establish building level funding. An example of a needed adjustment would be for all-day special or remedial class circumstances where very low pupil/staff ratios are the rule. Occasionally, a small group is scheduled into numerous regular classes but only for a fraction of a day or week. Such adaptability does not require weighting of pupil expenditure units since the basic allocation for all pupils should accommodate individualized pupil requirements. But when a special education class houses one-third or one-half the number of pupils as a regular classroon, a proportionately increased funding allocation is required. The amount is best determined by synthesizing all the building level costs required to operate each such class. The simulation should assume that this class is to be separately added to a school building. As such, it might require 2.75 of classroom teacher involvement, (calculated by comparing the special class size requirement of eight to the district class size average of twenty-two). Those eight pupils might also require .1 of the time of a school counselor, .1 of the time of the school speech and hearing therapist. and .4 of the regular building teachers' time when pupils are mainstreamed throughout the building. If a larger number of such classes are assigned to a single building, their impact on the school administrative and operational services might be determined and added to the pupil weighting funding formula. If when all such components are assembled, each special education student of a particular classification might require 3.75

units of personnel services, that weighting should be assigned to each school having such classes. It does not matter whether the students are from the school service area or are assigned into a particular building. If state-wide weightings for handicapped students are promulgated, they may be used intact or factored to accommodate local circumstances.

Otherwise, locally developed (system-wide) special pupil expenditure unit weightings are required. Table 4.1 shows the weighting system developed by a typical school system.

If it is a school district's policy to keep special education programs as a centrally directed and administered activity, all the costs of special education may be kept within the non-site basic section of the budget. In that case, classes may be attached to specific schools rather than assigned as a building level responsibility. There are considerations for each such method of operation. Central control assures an equality of effort, response, and adherence to prescribed mandates. It also places the classes within a school on a guest basis; overlooking opportunities for genuine "least restrictive alternatives" as special education legislation prescribes. If special education classes are administered at each location by on-site building leaders, there is apt to be a variance of equality of effort and results. Concomitant with that however, is the potential for innovative adaptive operations to improve both the classroom activities and meaningful integration into the school's overall activities.

For some borderline special education activities, schools can be guided into tutorial service programs by assigning premium incentive funding weightings to encourage the delivery of necessary services.

Occasionally schools will house separately funded instructional projects where in-kind services are required as a part of the grant package. In such cases, a pupil expenditure weighting should be provided for the school to assure that the regular program funding is not being diluted to accommodate a special tenant program. Such weightings may only require a small decimal equivalent, but they should be applied if equity of fund assignment is to be a defensible concept.

64

TABLE 4.1

EXCEPTIONAL PUPIL EXPENDITURE WEIGHTINGS

	SIMULATED UNIT VALUE	ELEMENTARY					JUNIOR HIGH							SENIOR HIGH			
		P.S.S.	E.M.	I.L.D.	L.D.R.	E.M.	E.M.R.	L.D.R.	C.L.D.	E.M.	E.M.R.	L.D.R.	T.M.R.	E.M.	E.M.R.	L.D.R.	T.M.R.
SPECIAL ED. TEACHERS	21,945	1	1	1	1	1	1	1	2	1	1	1	1	1	1	1	1
SPECIAL ED. AIDES	7,993	1	1	1			1	1	1				1	.50	1	.5	1
COUNSELORS	21,945			1			1		1					.50	1	1	1
SCHOOL PSYCHOLOGISTS	27,435	.14	.14	.10	.05	.08	.10	.10	.05	.10	.08			.24	.12	.24	.12
READING TEACHERS	21,945		.014	.014	.014	.014	.014	.014		.08	.04			.08	.04	.08	.04
SPEECH, LANGUAGE, HEAR. TEACHERS	21,945		.014	.01	.05	.01	.014	.014		.28	.01			.01	.02	.02	.01
MAINSTREAM TEACHERS	21,945	.20	.32	.16	1.3	.28	.28	1.5	.10	.42	.10	1.5		.42	.60	1.5	.20
TEXT & MATERIALS	450	1	1	1	1	1	1	1	1	1	1	1	1	1	1	1	1
SUMMARY OF COSTS		40,374	41,559	37,169	53,700	44,433	43,972	61,380	64,162	43,509				55,891		69,404	40,263
CLASS SIZE		12	7	10	20	7	10	20	10	12				15		25	8
SIMULATED COST/PUPIL		3,365	5,937	3,717	2,685	6,348	4,397	3,069	6,416	3,626				3,726		2,776	5,033
WEIGHTED PUPIL EXPENDITURE UNITS		2.1	3.7	2.3	1.7	3.9	2.7	1.9	3.9	2.2				2.3		1.7	3.1

P.S.S.   PRE SCHOOL SPECIAL   E.M.   EMOTIONAL MALADJUSTED   I.L.D.   INTERMEDIATE LEARNING DISABLED

L.D.R.   LEARNING DISABLED RESOURCE   C.L.D.   COMBINED LEARN. DISABLED   E.M.R.   EDUCABLE MENTALLY RETARDED

                                           T.M.R.   TRAINABLE MENTALLY RETARDED

Factoring for School Size. When schools are costed out on an individual basis, some variance may be attributed to size. A large school could distribute costs over a wide base. Until such time that additional supervisory or administrative help would be required, the larger school could be more cost efficient. The costs which contribute to cost efficiency are those that do not significantly vary with changes in pupil population. The building level costs which are prevalent, regardless of school size include administrative, clerical, and custodial service costs. In some schools the list could be expanded to include health services, library services, attendance services, or some special itinerant subject matter specialists.

If neighborhood schools are desired and extensive re-districting is to be avoided, it is possible to assign extra funds to smaller local schools yet still maintain a nexus of equity. It could be argued that some support for administrative, clerical, and custodial services would enable any school to remain as a viable enterprise, assuming pupil distributions and class size groupings would be acceptable. One such size support formula can be developed by measuring the impact of certain core costs associated with operating a school (administrative, clerical, and custodial salaries), and determining the student per capita costs of such services in the median school of the district. Then, all buildings having less than the median enrollment would be assigned equivalent per capita dollars to match the burdens of the median school. An equalized effort would then be possible for all the schools to provide the three services with no greater strain than the median school's effort. Such support should be identified and labled as a size subsidy.

Though rare, funds could be designated within a pupil weighting allocation system to promote desired changes. If, for example, a group, level, or type of student was to be targeted for special treatment, the pupil weighting allocations could be altered. Such coercions might be brought about because of previous neglect, acknowledged deficiencies, or recognized expansion requirements. The inherent flexibility within the school site budgeting process allows for such motivation. Schools can be encouraged to provide specific services by receiving some funds on a set-aside basis. If, for example, it was a central goal that schools must provide improved instruction in map reading skills each building could be assigned a separate per capita allocation which could only be used for the purchase of contemporary maps, globes, and charts, or similar paraphernalia. Such specialized funding thrusts are early decisions, made prior to dividing the available funds of the school pool.

By way of summary, school allocations are determined by a series of pupil expenditure units. First the raw number of pupils is factored for (kindergarten, elementary, secondary) grade level. Next, special education students are assigned weightings according to the specific needs of their handicaps. Then, special grant programs may receive special weightings for supplanted services. Finally, weightings may be made for small school units.

Per Pupil Unit Calculation. When all premium factors have been assigned, the total number of weighted per pupil expenditure units of the entire school system is summarized and divided into the school funding pool to establish the value of each such unit. The funded units are then assigned to school buildings in a lump sum for use in formulating a complete budget plan for the upcoming fiscal year. An illustration of unit allocations is provided in Table 4.2.

Determining Salary Costs. School site budgeting incorporates district-wide average salaries for all budgeting simulations. By dealing only with the average salaries, each school can achieve synthesized staffing units of equalized value throughout the school system. After all schools have completed their budget plans, the total number of positions in each employee category is re-assembled and adjustments made to the system-wide personnel complement. This method avoids issues of age, educational preparation, seniority, and wage levels of staff members assigned to each building. Such assignments may then be made on the basis of educational contributions rather than salary requirements. There is little evidence relating teacher instructional performance to salary received. Similar logic would prevail for administrators and supervisors, secretaries and clerical workers, para-professionals, and custodians.

Shools are provided with a list of average salaries and fringe benefits for each class of employee. Employee salary averages should reflect groupings for like positions; 12 month, 10½ month,

TABLE 4.2

ASSIGNMENT OF SCHOOL FUNDS

					BUDGET TARGET	22,567,840
					LESS BASIC COSTS	(6,149,860)
					ALLOCATION TO SCHOOLS	$16,437,980

SCHOOL	ENROLLMENT	WEIGHTED GRADE LEVEL *	EXCEPTIONAL PUPILS	WEIGHTED EXCEPTIONAL PUPILS **	WEIGHTED PUPIL EXPENDITURE UNITS	X $1643.27	SIZE SUBSIDY	ALLOCATION
ADAMS	298	279	22	43	322	529,136	136	529,272
BUCHANAN	233	220.5	23	46.5	267	438,756	7,350	446,106
FILLMORE	257	236.5	19	36.35	272.85	448,369	6,554	454,923
HARRISON	324	303.5	28	72.8	376.3	618,366		618,366
JACKSON	381	360	47	75.6	435.6	715,812		715,812
JEFFERSON	247	233	14	17.7	250.7	411,970	9,569	421,539
MCKINLEY	366	345	16	26.55	371.55	610,560		610,560
PIERCE	300	283.5	21	48.95	332.45	546,308		546,308
POLK	270	253.5	24	48.55	302.05	496,353	2,579	498,932
TAYLOR	312	293	14	23.25	316.25	519,687	647	520,334
TYLER	258	246	30	57.35	303.35	498,489	2,402	500,891
VAN BUREN	365	349	18	29.15	378.15	621,406		621,406
MADISON JR.HI.	647	769.93	55	134.95	904.88	1,486,969		1,486,969
MONROE JR. HI.	645	767.55	57	146.4	913.95	1,501,874		1,501,874
LINCOLN HI.	1,503	1,833.66	102	212.37	2,046.03	3,362,180		3,362,180
WASHINGTON HI.	1,841	1,880.02	129	252.76	2,132.78	3,504,733		3,504,733
ALTERNATIVE SCHOOL	50	59.5			59.5	97,775		97,775
					9,985.39	$16,408,743	$29,237	$16,437,980

68

grade level differences, shared time administrative/ teaching assignments, or differences provided for supervision. A sample list of average salaries and benefits appears as Table 4.3.

Fringe benefits are calculated on the basis of average costs for each group of employees. Some fringe benefits are charged on a per capita basis while some others are predicated on salary levels. Benefits are apt to vary between groups because of collectively bargained contractual variations. Fringe benefit averages are calculated by adding all costs for a like group and dividing the total cost by the number of like employees within the group. A grouping should consist of the same members assembled for average salary computational purposes. Schools use such average salaries and fringe costs to plan personnel costs within their total allocations. Whatever funds remain after salaries may be utilized for supplies, materials, or purchased services. In practice, more than 90% of a school's allocation will be required for the funding of salaries.

As previously mentioned, future salary averages may not be available at budget building time. The collective bargaining process may not have been completed. In such a case, two options are available. Salaries may be entered at the current year averages and an anticipated salary supplementary amount may be placed in a wage reserve in the basic cost section of the budget. Or, if a truer school cost representation is desired, the reserve for collectively bargained salaries may be applied to the total wage pool and added to the per capita average salary simulations. Wage reserves for collective bargaining may not reflect the eventual settlement amounts. Later adjustments are easily handled within the school site budgeting process since they will most likely be in a lump sum fashion.

All personnel costs must be expressed in terms of the average salary of each type of employee. Whether schools increase or decrease the number of positions in any category, the posted averages must be used. Schools may budget for less than a full position. Partial positions should be expressed as decimal equivalents. The tenths of positions may reflect portions of a full daily schedule or a share of a weekly schedule. If, for example, a position was budgeted for .2 it would reflect service for one day a week or one hour a day, each day. Ultimately all such fractional positions

Table 4.3 Simulated (average) Salaries For Budgetary Planning

Positions	Simulated Salaries	Benefits	Total
Aides, Educational	5,875	1,960	7,835
Counselors	22,831	3,425	26,256
Custodians, Regular	10,342	3,325	13,757
Head Cust., Elem. School	12,435	3,722	16,157
Head Cust., Sec. School	14,330	4,097	18,427
Principals, High School	32,478	4,872	37,350
Jr. High School	32,036	4,805	36,841
Elem. School	27,643	4,146	31,789
Asst. Principals, Hi. School	26,929	4,040	30,969
Jr. High	25,738	3,86L	29,599
Elementary	24,994	3,749	28,743
Program Coordinators	22,873	3,431	26,304
School Psychologists	23,510	3,527	27,037
Secretaries, 12 month	11,330	3,240	14,570
Secretaries, School Year	8,670	2,718	11,388
Teachers & Specialists	18,620	2,793	21,413

Hourly Services

Extra Secretarial	4.00 hourly
Extra Custodians	4.50 hourly
Utility Assistance	3.27 hourly

Other Rates

Substitutes, Professional	30.00 daily

are accumulated and personnel are assigned to various schools as required to produce a full employment schedule.

Collectively bargained agreements often require full fringe benefits for all employees who work at least half a schedule. Thus, two half time positions would require a double funding of fringe benefits. Such a doubling may be offest by the employment of several less than half time positions to fill other schedule requirements. If the discrepancy appears to be in one direction only, the cost effect should be acknowledged and accommodated when the budget is finalized.

Testing Potential Allocations. Having established the value of each pupil weighting and assigned those funds to schools, it is essential that the school appropriations be tested for adequacy. Since the intended appropriation will become the life line of the school it should be established that it will indeed support the school's activities. The fluid nature of assigning funds based on weighted assumptions might allow the school appropriations to become erroneous in any given year.

The adequacy of school appropriations may be examined by simulating a budget for schools at several funding levels. By applying the average salaries to accommodate the prescribed enrollment, an accurate indicator of adequacy of funding may be attained. It's not essential to synthesize the planning of all materials and supplies. It will suffice to estimate salary costs and acknowledge the remainder as a lump sum destined to provide for all goods and services.

If it is found that insufficient funds remain, several choices may be made. The basic cost section of the budget may be reviewed and reduced, thus freeing funds for the schools' funding pool. Or, the initial assumption regarding a total system funding limit may be raised. A third possibility would be to adjust the weightings to gain a better distribution of funds to various school levels. Finally, some school costs could be returned to the basic cost section of the budget if it could be shown that those tasks could be centrally achieved at significant cost savings.

At this juncture the effect of reducing the number

of school buildings could best be assessed. The net
costs of school closings can easily be simulated
when all salary and basic costs have been determined.
One measure of the attractiveness of school site
budgeting is its ability to lay out costs in an understandable fashion for easy manipulation and cost syn-
theses. It can equally accommodate planning for increased or decreased pupil populations, additions or
deletions of school plant, and expansion or reduction
of staff. All such calculations are concluded as a
planning model. A pro forma analysis of the assumed
situations allows analysis of the effect of each
changed circumstance or condition.

When all such studies have been completed and the
central administrative group is satisfied that schools
will be properly funded under the adopted formula, the
schools are given the raw data needed for budget planning: enrollment expectations, pupil weightings,
average salaries of staff, and total appropriations.
Each school may commence the planning of how such funds
may best be utilized to meet their local educational
needs during the upcoming budget period. To preserve
the fidelity of the school site budgeting process,
further adjustments to individual school appropriations
should be discouraged. It is essential that the intended equality of opportunity not be subverted to singular
school bids for arbitrary additional funding. Clear
cut cases of oversight should be judiciously resolved,
but not at the cost of system-wide parity. Remedial
actions should compensate only for obvious hardships.

Schools Create Budgets

Given all the raw ingredients, school leaders
commence to put together a spending package. The first
consideration involves the pupils to be served. How
will they be grouped for instruction? By trying several different assignment groupings, building leaders can
evaluate the relative merits of each configuration.
Class sizes contribute to pupil/teacher ratios which
in turn are the largest determinant of school costs.
But local schools have a choice of how best to staff
to meet their particular pupil needs. Options include
a team approach to instruction, split or combination
grade assignments, supplemental teaching assistance for
a portion of a school day, the employment of para-professionals, or the acqusition of sophisticated teaching

devices. The planning process continues to assign available funds as each such staffing decision is developed on a trial basis. Such decisions are best made at a school building level where the characteristics of the teaching staff can best be aligned with the peculiar needs of the students. The impetus of past practice and available supplementary resources may also become part of a school building's staffing decisions. With very little effort the outcome of many different staffing combinations may be evaluated as part of the planning process.

Soon after the local planning process is under way, the element of competition for funds causes an urgency for value analysis. Healthy competition, or as one superintendent describes it, "constructive tension" helps challenge the validity of each budgetary assumption. A balance of personnel and material needs must evolve from such competition. A healthful venting of priorities is apt to occur as progress towards instructional objectives is planned in an orderly fashion.

This provides an opportunity for genuine staff participation in making decisions that will affect their future. Professionally they may have to choose between optimum educational advantage for the students and other economic pressures for budgetary appropriations. Such decisions may challenge collectively bargained labor agreements or may cause the examination of mediocre programs whose pedigree is rooted in tradition. Given a clean slate, professional staff members may be a fountain of new or improved programs. In some schools, students have been invited to participate in planning for future school happenings.

School site budgeting begs parent and community input. Its reason for being is to accommodate local needs. School building leaders may seek parent input through budget planning sessions, regularly scheduled school-community business meetings, by questionnaires and opinion polls, from individual conferences, or from the creation of a school suggestion box. Whatever method is employed, a local school is likely to have a more acceptable community program if parents and other citizens of the community have had a voice in the establishment of school program priorities. This is not to imply a relinquishing of professional guidance to a rump caucus. The opportunity for a majority vote is contraindicated since minority views must also be accommodated, though they sometimes seem to be mutually exclusive.

Having received budget planning suggestions from staff, students, parents, and possibly central office administrators and employee labor groups, the school building administrator must examine the available alternatives and select those that best enable the local school to meet the district-wide instructional objectives. That criterion is the final basis for choice!

Having arrived at such decisions, the intended goal accomplishments should be specified and subject to public review. When the school budget is forwarded to higher authority for inclusion in the district budget plan, it should solidly represent the aspirations of its clientele. The budget document should contain all the requisite financial data and the goal statements of the expectations and changes to be enacted as a result of the school based management decisions.

Review by Central Office Group. A review of each school's budget submission provides the superintendent of schools with complete information concerning the manner in which district objectives are to be aided. Tests of adequacy, equity, and suitability reveal the completeness of each school's planning efforts. Conformity with district policies is another test made by the central review authority. Each budget must be examined for compliance with collectively bargained labor agreements, particularly for staffing levels, past practice clauses, and conditions of employment. Potential contractual violations can best be resolved by early analysis and remedial or avoidance measures. It is also possible to initiate a deliberate challenge, testing, or modification of contractual implications through provisions of a single school budget proposal.

School budget plans must be brought into line with statutes which prescribe instructional mandates, health and safety requirements, and recently emerging tests of accountability, achievement, or competency testing programs.

Another aspect of the central review process focuses on system-wide perspective. Unilateral actions, damaging to district goals, must be modified. Certain centrally prescribed mandates (pupil attendance, grade reporting and promotion, salary schedules, accounting and reporting, employee benefits) must be upheld.

After assuring concordance with all such house-keeping requirements, the central office review authority may examine the degree to which each local budget plan will contribute to the district's instructional objectives. Often, a very valuable pollination of ideas occurs. The central reviewer may cite the unique solutions of one school for the edification of each other school. Such idea sharing magnifies some of the advantages of the school site budgeting process.

Experienced reviewers will also be alert to errors or omissions when school site budgets are being processed. Graphic analysis and/or statistical compilation will quickly reveal planning discrepancies in any school's budget. Secondarily, such tests will validate the balanced judgements made by the schools. Extreme variances in salaries, materials, or services would surface for review.

The prime purpose for having the school budgets reviewed by a central authority is to assure that each school has met its obligation to its constituents! In so doing, the school has examined the needs of each student and provided compensatory responses to promote the fulfillment of district-wide instructional objectives. Each student will receive an equivalent educational opportunity.

Presentation to Board of Education. The Board of Education is provided with a budget in two parts, (1) the basic (non-site) centralized cost items, and (2) the individual school budgets. Together they represent the entire school funding proposal, assembled according to the best conceived notions of hundreds or thousands of people. The Board is directed towards a review of those elements which are destined to further the Board's district-wide educational outcomes. Ideally, each school unit has a place in the sun as budgetary plans are reviewed. In so doing, reference is made to previous successes and unmet needs, contemporary problems, and future remedial and progressive activities. The school budgets are assembled according to each instructional program within a building in order that the Board may assimilate the information in a coherent manner.

It is helpful if a few summary indicators are provided for easier analysis. Such summaries would show the total per pupil expenditure proposed for the teaching staff, for supplies and materials, and possibly the combined cost for each grade level and/or program. Uniform budget compilation and report forms should be used in order that reviewers can gather information efficiently and that the information has comparability with other schools. In addition to the numeric expenditure proposal, each school should provide a single page appendage highlighting program changes and improvements. Often a separate personnel summary sheet is also provided for instant analysis and comparisons. At the level of review by the Board of Education, an executive summary format best provides the right amount of information for the Board's understanding and enactment.

Conversion to Funding Format

Having the budget cast in an instructional program format, while most useful for in-house understanding and review, may not satisfy the legally prescribed form which the education appropriation must adhere to for legislative funding. By pre-planning, the data may readily be re-assembled in the mandated manner. Such conversions are available from microcomputers or a central data processing facility, providing the entry data were classified and coded for the various sort options. Currently, most legislative reviewers seem to utilize a form of line-item budget format. Their perspective is that public policy can best be served by minute exposure of each unit of expenditure. With data processing capabilities, legislators may be inundated with such data, prepared quickly and in high volume, making human review and comprehension very unlikely. One practical solution would be that of providing the legislatively required format and supplementing it with the school program information which evolved during the school site budgeting process.

It should be noted that the entire school site budgeting process is only a manner of planning for the assignment and distribution of resources. As soon as the district's educational appropriation is received, the school site compilations are abandoned and the overall budget is re-cast in the legally prescribed accounting format. Such format may still show costs by schools BUT all such entries will be in real salary costs, not simulated averages used for planning purposes.

If properly accomplished, the actual salaries, when assigned to all programs, grade levels, divisions, or school buildings will total to the salary base from which the average salaries were earlier derived. Thus the schools have added, subtracted, traded, and modified <u>positions</u> without the bias of the personalities occupying such positions. It was a simulating experience...

Chapter 5

ESTABLISHING NON-SITE COSTS

After selecting the overall budget target for the school district, the basic operating costs (which are not assignable to schools) need to be compiled. Being the first order of assignment does not mean that such funds are skimmed without regard to justification and consensus of allocation. A critical review process will take place wherein the schools will be given an opportunity to critique the basic cost proposal. Since all other allocations are to be made in the common denominator of pupil enrollment, this non-conforming assignation of funds takes place first in order to leave a large single block of funds for building allotments.

It bears repeating that basic (non-site) costs should continually be scrutinized to see whether they should be apportioned back to school buildings and incorporated within their budgets. The test is one of where the activity can BEST be accomplished - whether system wide perspective is required - whether the activity is beyond the capabilities of a single school building's sphere of control. Such items seem to deal with the support of instructional activities rather than direct participation therein. Some school observers might use the term "overhead" to register concern for any large amount of money set aside for the central direction of a school district. Yet, without positive leadership, a group becomes a mob. A well orchestrated school system provides services efficiently, effectively, and harmoniously as a result of well conceived top level direction.

Central Administrative Unit Costs

In a sense, the central administrative unit of a school district resembles a separate school cost center. There's a series of objectives that will be accomplished through the assignment of personnel, materials, and processes. Key objectives include the regulation of separate school buildings, the implementation of instructional happenings, the growth and development of students, the logistical and financial support of schools, the maintenance of intergovernmental relations, a variety of staffing concerns, and responsiveness to the school publics.

Expenses of the superintendent's office, the district business office, the instructional services office, and all subrogate divisions are funded in the basic (non-site) budget proposal.

Many central office activities are performed in response to legislated decrees. For example, activities associated with pupil accounting stem from legislation designed to assure pupil attendance at school rather than being employed in agriculture or industry. Most states require school districts to maintain minimum standards regarding length of school day and number of annual days of school offerings, curriculum offerings, professional certification, financial accounting and reporting, the care and custody of school properties, and more recently, measures of pupil achievement. These important activities require a funding level consistent with their purpose.

Another vital function of a central office school support facility is the matter of intergovernmental relations. Schools, as a government service, need to effectively relate to other governmental agencies in order to present school issues for full and fair consideration. In some instances schools are apt to be wholly dependent on other governmental bodies for such services as health, police and fire protection, and some pupil welfare services. There are shared programs wherein schools and municipalities develop workable relationships in such matters as community education, recreation, or cooperative use of school facilities. There's a third category of municipal relationships where schools are likely to furnish services to other governmental units through such avenues as school busing, census enumeration, cooperative purchasing, and certain child benefit services to non-public schools. School district administrative offices tend to seek, obtain, administer, husband, evaluate, and report the use of all the resources attained from multi-levels of government.

Often, the salary of a person to seek out and to process special funded grants can be recovered from those sources. But, that salary would initially appear in the basic cost section of the budget.

The paramount purpose of a central administrative unit is to provide system wide perspective and act as an adhesive to produce a cohesive instructional program without voids or gaps, excessive build-ups, or wasteful redundancies. As such, the central unit acts as a separate site requiring funding, not necessarily on a pupil per capita basis. When initially converting to school site budgeting, historical precedence may be the best point of departure when allocating funds for central administrative activities. If the central office has been adequately staffed, the initiation of school site budgeting should neither expand or diminish the level of existing staff positions. The decentralization of fiscal matters will shed some formerly centralized planning activity, but will simultaneously require additional school monitoring activity. A system of data processing services is essential in order to accommodate the explosion of accounting information generated by the separate schools.

A list of funding requirements to carry out centrally directed functions might include:

Supervision
Program Planning
Census and Pupil Enumeration
Attendance and Pupil Records
Personnel Relations
Business Functions
Evaluation
Staff Development
Research and Testing
Retirement Incentives
Employee Benefits
Administrative and Clerical
Inter-School Travel Reimbursement
Financial Management

School Support Activities

A second category of non-site funding requirements within the basic cost section would provide for pooled school support activities. Often, a single school would be too small an entity to support such costs, but by banding together, large volume savings are incurred and improved services are provided. A prime example would be that of data processing services. While each school obtains a full range of services, including student scheduling and financial and personnel reports, the cost of operating a data center is not controllable, affordable, or assignable to a single school user. Hence, it is properly described as a school support cost that is being harbored in the basic cost section. If desirable, the cost of such services can be back-charged or distributed to schools, departments, or agencies on the basis of services rendered. For matters of strict cost analysis and cost/benefit controls, such parcelling of costs may be essential. But most often such procedures reflect a distribution of current or prior operations rather than a budget planning or model simulation tool.

Some other entities, on the basis of economy of scale, could best be handled within the basic costs set-aside: warehousing activities, instructional materials centers, a printing center, in-house specialty repair services, and some pooled risk insurance coverage. The upkeep of a central postage processing center should be a basic cost element. However, postage usage is a controllable school site budgeting obligation.

A case could be made for or against the removal of fuel and utilities (water, phones, power) from the school site cost segment to the basic costs budget section. Remembering the concept of providing equal opportunities on the basis of student enrollment, fuel and utility costs could skew equalization efforts unless statistically treated. The fuel supply of a school building would be related to the building's age and size and the design of the heating, ventilating, and air handling systems within the structure. Different energy sources may be found in separate schools. Some schools may use more than one energy source, while others may have the capability of alternately switching energy sources based on economic factors or availability of supply. If a posture is assumed that such variations are more subject to chance (largely because of the variable physical plants in a school district), the fuel (energy) costs would be assigned to the basic cost budget. Or, the opposite approach would enable school leaders to say that fuel and utility costs, even though mostly affected by building conditions, are yet highly predictable on a historic per capita basis. As such, they should be part of a school site budget but equalized (weighted) to compensate for building characteristics. There should still be the incentive of performance improvement based on historic averages. In this case, all utilities of the school district would first be pooled and then proportionately parcelled back to schools with performance targets centrally (but cooperatively) established.

In periods of rapidly escalating fuel and electricity costs, it may be better to keep such costs in the basic budget section, assuming cost overruns can be met through supplemental appropriations, transfer of contingent funds, or some pooling of resources. If escalation took place when fuel and utilities were designated within a school budget, the school would then have to fund the increases from a very limited option base, most likely affecting an instructional allocation. Perhaps the method to accomplish all such ends is that of relegating fuel and utility costs to the central basic budget and establishing historical preformance norms for each school. Normally such norms are propogated on the basis of a five year rolling average factored for degree-day heating and cooling demands. Thus, if a school unexplainedly fails to meet consumption goals, the school budget can be assessed the make-up costs. Such obligations might even carry over to subsequent fiscal years if unable to be met in the year of default. But, if consumption targets are bettered, the schools might share some largesse. If consumption goals are achieved but rapidly rising costs require substantially increased financial appropriations, it should be noted that the basic cost budget section can best spread the increase over a larger base or seek other funding sources.

Another school support cost is incurred by school transportation activities. The amount of transportation to and from any school is mostly determined by the chance distribution of pupil population and often affected by local hazardous conditions. Differing schools within a district may have significantly differing school transportation demands. Being remote of instructional activities, the cost of such a variable commodity should not displace school site funds available for instructional purposes. It would cause a disequalizing effect. Hence, basic transportation, being provided in response to a state mandated and/or a district wide policy, is best assigned to the basic cost section of the budget. Optional transportation, such as for field trips, athletic contests, or extracurricular activities, would be obtained with school site funds set aside at the option of the building budget planners.

While each school plans and implements the best

accommodation of district wide educational objectives,
they also will separately purchase the particular
materials required to match their content and mode of
instruction. This results in numerous single purchase
transactions which are more costly then large volume
buying. To help abate such added costs, many common
supply items can be purchased in large volume and either
locally warehoused or shipped directly to each consumer.
Goods purchased on the basis of large volume competitive
bidding will cost less, and with planning will be on
hand and available when needed. There's a third advantage in being able to sample and test large volume
orders; assuring quality standards. Volume purchasing
procedures may be applied for art, general, and paper
supplies; custodian and cleaning supplies; physical
education, science, and industrial arts supplies; and
printed forms. The schools not only save the paper
work of ordering all such materials, they benefit from
their ready and uniform availability. The costs of
such common supplies may be initially budgeted within
basic costs and centrally warehoused. If so, the value
of goods shipped to each school is subsequently back-
charged. School allocations need to be established on
a per capita basis. The overhead of warehousing costs
would remain as a basic cost. Another way of setting up
such large volume savings would be to have each school
set aside a pre-determined allocation to be used for
centralized purchasing of common items. The disadvantage of assessing each school a specified amount is the
likelihood of building level overstocking with unused
goods. Conversely, if set up within a drawing account,
initially funded in the basic cost budget section, the
stock will remain in common storage, rotated to assure
freshness, and not stockpiled in numerous buildings.
Thus, schools that economize can have unused dollars
for other purposes while schools that exceed their
draw allowance will be required to divert other funds
to pay for their extravagance.

Reserve Accounts

The basic cost section of a budget can be used
as a repository for funds which at a later point in
time will be assigned or parcelled elsewhere. If,
for example, at budget making time there are still
unresolved labor issues and the collective bargaining
process has not been completed, a sum estimated to
cover emerging settlements can be assigned to a reserve

status within the basic costs budget. In order to mask management's settlement estimate (a desirable tactic in negotiations) monies for several proposed future obligations can be amalgamated in an unidentifiable fashion.

A funded reserve to accommodate enrollment projection deviations is another entity assigned to the basic costs budget. Since budgetary planning precedes the start of a fiscal year by as much as ten months, variations between projected and actual September enrollments require that schools be given a correction factor for funds assigned on a per capita basis. Such make-up funding becomes important when enrollment exceeds projections and additional classes must be formed. The attendant funding can be attained from an enrollment projection correction fund within the basic costs. If the enrollment error is in the other direction (over-estimated) it may be possible to transfer the resources of a class to a different school having an opposite (underestimated) enrollment situation. In both cases, good data are needed instantaneously in September to minimize the disruptions of cancelling, formulating, or regrouping classes of students. Where enrollment projections are only slightly in error, schools may be compensated by assigning such extra funds as required for supplies, books, and materials, assuming the randomly distributed excess pupils can be accommodated with existing staff. Again, such supplemental funds are available within this reserve account.

A reserve account may be set up in the basic costs budget to provide funding for program improvements, research, testing, or pilot programs: things not wholly affordable or supportable by a single school building. A criticism of the school site budgeting process is that it fosters a status quo syndrome by only funding day to day activities. A reserve account provides a centralized funding for growth and improvement activities. There is not a wall of separation between centrally sponsored and school participatory program improvement efforts. However, when new programs have passed the experimental or pilot stage and are adopted within district-wide instructional objectives, they become obligatory for the schools to fund, though sometimes by displacing other program components.

While each school sets aside an allowance for the ordinary absences of staff members, long term absences need to be re-insured within the basic costs section of the budget. If experience shows that the average absentee rate is 4%, the schools should be prepared to fund replacements to that extent. A typical arrangement provides that after ten days of continuous absence, the replacement person's salary is charged to the centrally funded substitute reserve account. Such accounts are historically determined (and likely adjusted to reflect emerging statutory benefit rights of employees) and might ordinarily be funded at about 2% of each unit's total payroll. This reserve acts as a bank and in some districts it is funded by having employees, through collective bargaining, agree to donate some accrued leave privileges in order to set up such a bank to provide for extended benefits for catastrophic needs. It has been observed that when schools are placed on the incentive plan to fund the first days of absence, they often find ways of reducing the utilization of substitut employees. This is accomplished through some doubling o assignments, re-allocation of non-teaching assignments, student schedule modifications, or administrative pinch hitting.

Some earmarked funding grants may be temporarily assigned to the basic costs budget section. If so, they may subsequently be transferred to the unit where they are to take place. Their influence will thus not upset the per capita equalization thrust of school site budgeting. Where such grants are for general purposes and not restricted to a specific clientele, their value should be added to the gross amount available to schools and equally distributed at the time the gross appropriations are made for each school.

Another form of reserve account is the clearing account to accommodate staff attrition. In the normal course of replacing departing senior staff members with new inexperienced employees, a significant salary gain accrues. At budget planning time, such "turnover" accounts can be set up on a negative (suspense) anticipatory basis. As such attrition takes place the generated funds can be transferred into the account, eventually eliminating its deficit position.

Obligations incurred in prior years should be funded within the basic costs budget. If retirement incentive payments are spread over more than one fiscal year, their future obligations can be accommodated in this fashion. Or, if there are extended leave privileges requiring salary or benefit supplements, they too may be centrally funded in subsequent basic cost budgets.

If the school district provides support for non-school community programs such as municipal library, museum, park, zoological, or recreation programs, such contributions are assigned to basic costs rather than school site costs. Community and continuing educational programs are other examples of non-school site costs.

Concentrated Instructional Programs

The option exists to provide for special intensive instructional programs within the basic costs budget. This may be desirable (1) if their costs are very different from the normal funding designations, or (2) if they contain students introduced into a single building or class because of their unique need. For example, a class of severely mentally impaired students would require a very low pupil/teacher ratio, customized materials and furnishings, and added support staff. The host school of such a group would be dis-equally compensated if required to provide for the class from ordinary appropriations. One alternative is to keep the costs of all such special (intensive) education programs in the basic costs budget and to attach the class to a regular school, with all attendant costs paid. Similar arrangements might be made for other added cost explicit programs for gifted, vocationally oriented, or otherwise academically unique classes. When such classes are centrally budgeted, they would also be centrally designed and guided. If such an arrangement is not desirable, all such concentrated instructional programs can be pre-assigned to specific schools and a sufficient sum of added funding provided to compensate for their costs in excess of ordinary costs. The advantage of that alternative is to have such classes assimilated into the complete school kinship and to encourage daily decisions at the level which is best able to be aware of current needs and available responses. Further discussion of the management and fiscal support for concentrated instructional programs appears in Chapter 7.

Grouping Non-site Costs

Basic budget costs should be assembled in the locally established conventional budget format. If the community is accustomed to line item, function object, program, zero based, cost center, activitity, or charter based budget array, the basic budget document may adhere to the prescribed form. If, however, the introduction of school site budgeting (which is really a budget simulation rather than an official instrument) permits an optional grouping, it is recommended that basic costs be grouped by program/component, or function/object. This enables the creation of another dimension of school operational analysis. Ultimately as a measure of equalization, costs can be displayed by building and program within each school building. Further analysis can be made to show costs by class within a grade, if such were desired. The reader is reminded of the underlying thrust of school site budgeting; to provide equivalent educational opportunities for all students (and to validate that circumstance).

Improvement of Instruction

One portion of basic cost planning is aimed at evaluating and improving the instructional efforts of the schools. As a quality control device, it serves a central administration management goal. Expenditures may be planned for curriculum monitoring and planning, the in-service growth and development of teachers and administrators, research and data gathering expenses, program evaluation, and the process of infusing contemporary technology into schools.

Other instructional improvements are advanced through such centralized concerns as testing and grade reporting, student grouping and scheduling, matters of discipline and attendance, and promotional policies. All of these concerns require global perspective rather than single school building orientation, hence they are assigned to the basic cost (planning) section.

Reviewing Non-site Costs

When all basic needs as described herein have been converted to dollar values and assembled, it is necessary to have them exposed and accepted by the several constituent groups.

The superintendent of schools and central office staff should review the assembled costs for omissions, estimate validations, conformance to existing policies, regulations and statutes, cohesiveness, and relationship to adopted objectives. The subjective element of balance or apportionment is evaluated and a review of potential financial impact is completed. Adjustments may be indicated.

Next, the basic cost budget is presented to school building leaders for review. Their perspective acknowledges that funds set aside for basic costs tend to remove funds otherwise assignable to separate school buildings. They must also understand the relationship of central support services to their daily program needs. Their observations would focus on issues of adequacy, timeliness, availability, apportionment, redundancy, and effectiveness and efficiency of centrally provided basic services. In their consumer role, building leaders provide unique insight into the development of a basic cost budget. Again, adjustments may be indicated.

The third level of review of the basic budget proposal is provided by the Board of Education. That group is seeking a measure of progress, potential achievement, financial impact, program quality and improvement, and efficiency and effectiveness in carrying out prescribed policies and meeting adopted objectives. As earlier stated, the centrally developed basic cost budget resembles a school site budget, destined to work towards the accomplishment of specified objectives. In that role, the superintendent resembles a building leader and the school board acts as a counterpart to parents who participate in constructing school (building level) budgets.

Several axioms of developing a basic cost budget are worthy of repetition:

1.   Items in the basic cost budget are examined in order to get them relegated to school site budgets whenever feasible.

2.   The central administration of a school district has a series of pronounced activities to coordinate and coalesce the overall instructional effort.

3. Some things need to be provided by a central funding source due to economies of scale, availability of clerical services or specialized elements, and operational proficiency.

4. Some costs are not readily assignable to schools since their needs are randomly influenced by uncontrollable matters of geography, physical plant configuration, or composition of pupil population.

5. The basic cost section of the budget sometimes serves as a temporary repository of monies for eventual sequential assignment to schools, programs, staff, or a special clientele.

Basic costs need early identification and compilation since they require funding in advance of school allocations. A rule of thumb might show that basic costs assume 20% to 25% of a total school district budget. They are sometimes described as the glue that holds the school system together.

Chapter 6

DETERMINING SCHOOL ALLOCATIONS

After the typical 20-25% of the total allocation
target has been labeled for basic (non-site) costs,
attention can be turned to assigning bulk funding to
each school unit. For this breakdown, the classification and quantity of students determine the building
allotments. Funds are to be distributed on a pupil
per capita basis, but with different amounts (weighted
pupil expenditure units) assigned to differing categories of students.

Pupil Classifications

In the search for equity, the differing needs of
students must receive equally differing resources.
Remedial and tutorial programs must be provided for low
achievers. Enriching and challenging programs must be
provided for high achievers. Comprehensive and dynamic
programs must be provided for normal achievers. When
each is served according to need, an equitable educational opportunity is being provided. The charting or
tracking of resources to be provided to each student
is recorded in a financial plan or budget.

Some budgets are compiled in program or function-
object formats and may include statements of outcomes
or anticipated benefits. Other budget systems, such
as zero-based or activity budgeting, may illustrate
predetermined limits or expenditures intended to achieve
specific ends. School budgeting systems are most often
primarily designed to be fiscal monitors.

The first required estimate is that of gross enrollment to be housed at each building. Such an estimate may be determined by available census data combined with upgrading of present enrollees to include
graduation from upper grades and projections regarding
the size of incoming classes. Other considerations
include historical migration between grades, a review
of retention ratios, accelerated promotions, open
enrollment electives, a study of neighborhood dwelling
characteristics, the impact of other (non-public)
schools, construction of housing, migratory patterns,
and school program changes. The sum of these factors
provides a reasonable basis for reliably predicting
the total number of students anticipated at each grade

91

level. Computerized manipulation of such data provides
accurate and timely prognosis. Since pupil counts are
directly transformed into financial support allocations,
it is imperative that estimates are carefully derived.
If a community maintains an open enrollment policy
(students may attend the school of their choice without
regard to neighborhood boundaries), their elections need
to be made one year in advance in order that their
funding grant may be assigned to the proper school.

After accounting for all students of the district,
those who will not attend local schools may be identified and removed from the school rolls. The funding
for their attendance at non-district schools (career-
vocational, alternative, special program) would be
based on tuition costs and provided for in the basic
(non-site) section of the overall budget outline. It
is conceivable that some such students will be lured
back to district schools by the creation of specialized
programs of a similar nature. To encourage such transition of school programs, funding comparisons can be
made to show the costs and benefits of starting such
new programs at the home school. To assure regular
examination of such "make or buy" special programs,
funding costs might be assigned to local school buildings with the proviso that local building leaders regularly assess the probability of supplanting such non-
district placements by developing similar competitive
offerings.

Having arrived at the point of calculating the
net number of students to be accommodated in each
building, it is necessary to refine their make-up and
classify them according to learning needs and grade
level differentials.

Students with special educational needs require
extraordinary funding consignments to compensate for
their abnormalities. Typically there is a requirement for smaller class sizes, additional para-professional assistance, specialized materials, extensive
diagnostic procedures, a closer monitoring of progress,
and a flexible schedule of events. These inequalities
require special funding consideration if equivalent
educational opportunities are provided to ameliorate
their deficiencies. The standard share of pupil allocations would be grossly inadequate and might tend to
perpetuate their exceptional characteristics. A
series of weighted pupil expenditure units is employed.

To provide the desired educational programs, instructional models are constructed to show the configuration required for each classification of exceptional students. Chapter 7 describes the method of simulating and synthesizing suitable instructional programs for each category of exceptionality. Thus, as such students are assigned to individual school buildings, they are reinforced with a weighted expenditure unit count in order to provide the supplementary funding required. While a normal student of an elementary school may be supported by a net allocation of $1,800, an exceptional student requiring extensive remediation may require 1.5 or 2.5 times the base amount for instructional services. Local school districts are encouraged to formulate weightings for customized configurations of specialized instructional programs. Differentiation need not be limited to handicapped or gifted students. Variable funding assignments could be developed to facilitate and promote such divergent programs as business preparation, scientific studies, career and vocational, liberal arts, work study, alternative, or any specialized cost intensive offering. It is necessary to outline the requirements of the program, estimate average cost and time components, establish per capita costs, and relate those costs to the average program costs to arrive at an index or weighting factor. In this fashion, exceptional students or programs receive proportionately exceptional financial support required to provide for their disparate nature. If some such programs have categorical funding assistance provided by external sources, such monies should be deducted before pupil weighting assignments are established. If supplementary aid is of a general (non-directive) nature it should be added to the overall budget target and normally distributed through the fundamental allocation process.

Grade Weightings

To equalize educational support the elements of grade level costs need to be recognized. For example, if kindergarten programs are only conducted for half of a normal school day, such students should receive a grade level weighting of .5 or half the resource allocation of a full time student of other grades.

Elementary school students, in a regular classroom environment, become the bench mark or reference base from which weightings are established. Normally they receive a count of one (1).

Secondary school students in a regular program require additional funding because of smaller class groupings which require the employment of additional teachers, specialized equipment and materials support, the lesser efficient schedules produced by pupil mobility and elective offerings, and variable time assignments of teachers.

To determine the weighting factors to compensate for such situations requires an analysis of recent funding assignations prior to the implementation of school site budgeting. Depending on what costs are to be shown as being related to school buildings, vis a vis district-wide basic costs, the weighting for secondary school pupils is apt to range between 1.15 and 1.3 of elementary school expenditures. If schools are grouped in some sort of overlapping (middle school) pattern of organization, the weighting may be lower, more akin to an elementary school. Non-comprehensive or specialized schools may require a separate analysis to establish their historic expenditure requirements.

If there is consensus that prior funding assignments were not proper at all grade levels, it is timely to make adjustments at the start of the school site budgeting process. Or, after a few experience cycles of school site budgeting, provisions can be made to alter the grade level or specialized school weightings to effect desired outcomes. There is a considerable degree of versatility in the development of school site budgeting allocations. Planning techniques encompass model building and cost simulation procedures. Not only may enrollment change simulation be conducted, but changes of pupil expenditure unit weightings, special program options, or even a higher or lower level of financial support may be assumed in order to evaluate potential outcomes. Also, the effects of collective bargaining discussions can be quickly applied to average salary simulations to predict the total impact of such deliberations. The potential gains from employing para-professional staff members can be examined by developing models of variable staffing patterns. In short, school site budgeting can become a very convenient vehicle for "what if" models or postures.

The weighted pupil expenditure units are summarized. The total available allotment for schools is divided by the number of weighted pupil expenditure units to arrive

at the unit value of funds to be assigned to each
school. The value of each weighted pupil expenditure
unit will be less than the full per pupil cost of the
district, since it does not include those elements contained within the basic cost section of the planning
process. Nevertheless, it is a valuable unit for
planning purposes, especially when enrollment shifts are
to take place. If, for example, a school district is
faced with declining enrollment and the necessity to
close school buildings, the pupils may be transferred
to other buildings with their weighted expenditure units
intact. Or, if schools are to be opened to accommodate
expanding enrollment, the pupils and their attendant
allocations can be assigned to the new facilities.
Since costs are fully equated to enrollment, there is
a built in escalator to accommodate either declining,
expanding, or shifting pupil population.

Size Subsidies

In the quest for equality, some consideration
should be shown for the differing funding requirements
brought about by schools of varying size. Some fundamental building-associated costs are common to all
schools. Some operational costs tend to be a greater
burden to small schools which receive an amount of
funding based on their limited enrollment. For example, each school unit requires a core of administration, secretarial service, and custodial service.
Typically, a core staff contingent could effectively
handle a school of several hundred students. If their
salaries were supported by stipends of several hundred
students, their per capita impact would be nominal.
Conversely, if an equivalent staff were retained to
operate a building of half that enrollment, their
burden on per capita funding appropriations would be
doubled. Yet, for many reasons, it is highly desirable
to continue the operation of small school buildings
rather than terminate them for consideration of size
shortfalls.

One method for providing a subsidy for small
schools is to provide a supplemental appropriation
to help cover such fundamental costs. It could be
assumed that the school having the median enrollment
level could ideally afford the administrative, clerical,
and custodial staffing complement. By adding the
average salaries of these three entities and dividing

by the median enrollment, a per capita operational share is established. That rate is then provided to other schools for each pupil below the district median. For example, if the combined average salaries and fringe benefits for a principal, secretary, and custodian totaled $60,000 and the median school building enrollment of the district was 300 pupils, the amount of $200 of each pupils' stipend would be rendered for that purpose. A smaller school, perhaps housing 280 pupils would thus be subsidized by $4,000 (20 [below median] X $200). If desirable, a similar plan could be applied to larger schools to take away $200 per pupil for each pupil in excess of the median. In that fashion, a sparsity/density system of funding would have an equalizing effect on individual school allocations. This provides a better distribution of the burden of commonly essential services. Similar logic could be applied to any other factors that skew local school costs. Supplementary doles are made from the overall target, after basic costs have been established, but before pupil expenditure unit values are determined. The distribution among the schools is slightly changed by such a size equalization subsidy.

To Promote Change

The categorical appropriation of monies can be a decisive influence in shaping school happenings. Desired results can be achieved by channelling extra resources on a priority basis. Such earmarking may be used to promote remediation of acknowledged deficiencies strengthening of lesser efforts, the introductions of new programs, the acceleration of laggard programs, the enrichment of barren offerings, the desirability of either combining or splitting some components, or the consolidation of programs into differing configurations. All such changes can be brought about by and with the aid of directed funding allocations.

Another way to influence school direction is through the availability of incentive grants whereby schools may receive added monies for predetermined purposes: the development of new curriculum, the isolation of problems, the accommodation of the unusual needs of pupils, pilot programs having district-wide potential, differentiated staffing, in-service staff development activities, teaching strategies, and experimentation or essay. When incentive grants are assigned for such purposes, there is an implication that their expenditures will be isolated and their results capable of being monitored. In order to examine happenings and results, audit trails must be established for such designated funding. The combined input of school funds and incentive grant funds may be compared, contrasted, and confirmed, leading to cost-benefit review.

Some schools under certain circumstances may wish to allocate funds to other schools in a sub-contracting relationship. If specialized programs are available at near-by schools, it may be more economical to purchase the service on a tuition basis, rather than to tool up to provide a similar program. The school site budgeting process has the flexibility to permit and encourage the attainment of the best fit of assigned resources. The receiving school is then credited with funds from the sending school. Such "make or buy" decisions tend to reduce the proliferation of small, inefficient, redundant, specialized classes.

Within a building, a school leader may wish to assign funds based on enrollment or student electives, program value, staff availability, directional thrusts, or for purposes of remedial activities. Being careful not to establish costs as the prime determinant of program offerings, the building leader may nevertheless consider cost as one factor to be reviewed as a measure of equity.

Corrections and Adjustments

Since budget planning and preparation usually precedes the budget operational period by 6 to 18 months, it is likely that enrollment projections, the basis for fund allocation, will require adjustment. Otherwise, schools will be unjustly rewarded or penalized by being bound to obsolete assumptions. Further comlicating the issue is the general requirement that professional staff members be given 3 to 6 months (legalistic) notification of their retention or severance.

Having contractual commitments, it is troublesome to arrange last minute re-assignments, but that is exactly what must take place if enrollment so dictates. The shuffling of personnel tends to alter the budgetary planning models causing some schools to relinquish assets and others to gain unbudgeted staff members.

Since staff members were budget simulated at the prevailing average salary, there is little argument for
the assignation of personnel based on age, experience,
or biographical characteristics. Given that degree of
flexibility, persons may readily be transferred intradistrict to accommodate enrollment variations.

Minor variations between early enrollment projections and September actualities can generally be
accepted. A few students, more or less, normally
distributed, are not apt to trigger major concerns
unless contractually determined ceilings are violated.
However, an accumulation of students in a single grade
or class may require some adjustment. Building leaders
may make application to the reserve account of the
basic budget if additional (unbudgeted) personnel are
essential due to enrollment forecast discrepancies.
Schools are then provided with the necessary personnel
and the materials costs for extra students.

One way of providing for enrollment projection
errors is to arrange for the September transfer of a
pre-determined amount of money to provide supplies
and materials for excesses or shortfalls of student
population. A per capita supply/materials allocation
would accompany each child and be transferred to or
from schools as indicated. The gross difference may
be taken from or credited to the central (basic budget)
set-aside. In this manner, enrollment changes are
accommodated by (1) transferring personnel as warranted
and (2) providing fund adjustments for per-capita supply,
material needs of actualized enrollments. This tends
to recognize the constraints of adequate preliminary
planning without disturbing the equity of school allocations or violating contractual employment agreements.

School site budgeting attempts to achieve two
levels of equity in the assignation of funds to school
buildings. The first goal is to provide equal resources
to each student. The second goal is to provide supplemental resources as needed by atypical students. By
combining the initial allocation and the supplemental
resources, a school may offer an equivalent educational
opportunity for each pupil of the school and the
school district.

The reader may assume that the school site budgeting process, through the medium of assignment of funds,
is sufficiently flexible to permit and influence the

desired behavior of individual schools. Their performance can be elevated, deflated, accelerated, retarded, expanded, compressed, enlarged, or diminished by the assumptions made concerning assignment of funds to individual school buildings. All this is accomplished while simultaneously providing a high degree of building level autonomy. The allocation of funds to individual school buildings is a process that requires careful and thoughtful analysis, but it offers tremendous opportunities for getting a better fit of funds in relation to needs.

Chapter 7

FUNDING FOR EXCEPTIONAL PUPILS

The flexibility of the school site budgeting process provides many options concerning the degree of decentralization accorded the operation and management of programs for exceptional pupils. A case could be built for special education program direction to be (1) decentralized, (2) centralized, or (3) partially independent. Some of the trade-offs attendant to such a decision require an up-to-date point of view concerning what seems to be best for the designated pupils. There is a prevailing inclination that special education is not very different from general education, and there is a decided trend away from a perpetuation of remedial orientation towards more customary preventive and developmental programs. The broad category of behavioral disorders replaces singular labeling stigmata. Attitudinal problems are overcome as students are re-directed away from isolation into the mainstream of schools with only their disabilities separately diagnosed and attended. Local school districts may still opt to conduct some programs for exceptional pupils in fairly contained environments. Decisions need to be based on the type, number, and availability of students to be served, and often, the transportation needs associated with their geographical residence. In larger school districts providing multiple facility options, the issue of centralized or decentralized structuring may indeed be a clearer choice. The following discussion of management options serves to illustrate the facility with which school site budgeting can support or supplement any such administrative control variations.

Centralize or No

If assigned as part of the constituency of a local school building there is a higher probability of integration into all aspects of the schools' programs and staff services. Local schools would tend to absorb exceptional pupils and deal with their special needs as required. The specially trained personnel who operate the special classes would become a valued school resource in working with teachers of regular classes who may need assistance in coping with learning disorders of children not assigned to special classes. All the resources of the school would similarly be available to the special

101

class members. Unique and innovative responses, highly customized, would be directed to their daily needs. The likelihood of their being mainstreamed into normalized school activities, according to their individualized plans, would become routine. The impetus would be for local building leaders to apply equivalent efforts towards meeting their precise learning deficiency. The only constraints on the success of such a decentralized approach would be the capability of the local building leader, the enlightenment of the school community, the need for specialized diagnostic and progress monitoring procedures, and the competition for available in-house resources.

A case could likewise be built to support the concept of keeping special educational programs under a central authoritative direction and control, and to merely attach the classes to local school units. This would assure an equivalent delegation of resources to each such pupil and would have the effect of establishing district-wide quality program standards. The ease of transferrability of staff, students, or instructional paraphernalia would be evident. Some economies of scale may occur through centralized control. Also, funds designated for use in such classes would be readily isolated, accounted for, audited, and not diverted to or diluted by other needs. The drawbacks to a centralized operation of special educational programs are brought about by their impersonal attachment to larger schools. Their status as an appendix tends to perpetuate their isolation. Their tenant role excludes them from the host school climate. There is no interchange of resources. Their progress is only as good as the degree of centralized proficiency and competence which manages and directs their activities.

A third arrangement might include the best elements of both schemes - a partially decentralized assignment of special education classes. Some units of lesser handicapped clients can better succeed when assigned to a local school building, while groups of severely handicapped clients require a large amount of centralized support and might best function in the realm of being attached to a local school building. There may still be a third type of exceptionality that requires some groups of clients to be to be totally isolated from any school units and housed in an independent facility.

School site budgeting has the unique adaptability to accommodate any such arrangement or assignment of students requiring exceptional educational programs. The supplementary costs associated with each special need may be (1) simulated and constructed, (2) designated, and (3) transported with the student. If special (categorical) funding credits are provided by other sources, they may be included in establishing the funding packages for each unit.

Two other factors need to be studied when planning for the housing of exceptional educational programs. First is the child advocacy notion that pupils be placed in the least restrictive environment. In determining where that consequence may occur, a review of local circumstances is mandated. Consistent with the peculiar needs of the unit, the most normalized type of school environment is primarily warranted.

Secondly, the ongoing expenses of transporting pupils to specialized units needs to be considered. Except in densely populated urban districts, greater transportation distances will be required to convey students to sparsely assigned classes for exceptional pupils. Such added costs need to be factored when making special pupil or class assignments.

Wherever such units are assigned, particular local circumstances need to be evaluated. The administrative and academic climate of the host school needs to be appraised as well as the availability of space and the potential for adaptation of physical facilities. Conceivably such appendants might best succeed if generally isolated from the unit to which they are attached. Centralized know-how might produce the greatest benefits. Conversely, upon examination of local conditions, some units would thrive and grow as in a partnership relationship when assigned to a local school. Whichever arrangement is formulated, school site budgeting will equitably aid and abet such decisions. The least important determinant of unit locations should be that of mandated segregated accounting for and auditing of designated special funding appropriations. For even the most difficult case, contemporary data processing capabilities will isolate and monitor financial activities without regard to their assigned location or method of control. Assignments need to be exclusively based on pupil welfare.

Funding Provisions

If special classes are to be centrally operated, the funding provisions would become a part of the basic (non-site) section of a district's budget. In that case, all salaries would be projected at their actual cost rather than their simulated averages. All attendant costs such as employee benefits, travel reimbursements, professional growth activities, and supportive services need to be included in the centrally managed effort. When the classes are subsequently attached to a school building, they would be fiscally independent of the school and expect no instructional services from the building. If more than one such class is attached to a school, it would be necessary to furnish some additional funding to the school to compensate for school operational activities consumed by the attached classes. Such elements as custodial cleaning services, rest room supplies, telephone usage, library upkeep, utilities, health services, and mail and publications provisions should not be drained from the host school. Such a funding supplement (rent) could be pre-determined and credited to the host school at the time when class locations are fixed. The intent is to prevent the diversion of equalized local school expenditure allowances to non-local programs.

When special classes are assigned to local school buildings, the entire funding allowance is immediately credited to the school building's appropriation. The merged funding permits the school community to plan for the complete accommodation of the special classes.

Model Building

If the special classes have inordinate costs, a pro forma model of their financial needs may be constructed to provide the necessary level of support. Such a simulation for a class of Intermediate Learning Disabled students would show:

Class Size: 10
Salaries: Averaged

Teacher	1.0	$20,000
Aide	1.0	9,000
School Psychologist	.10	2,000
Reading Specialist	.014	280

Speech, Hearing, Lang. Spec.	.010	200
Regular Teachers	.16	3,200
Books and Materials		450
Class Cost:		$35,130
Per Capita Cost:		$ 3,513
District average per capita allowance:		$ 1,464
Weighted cost of ILD pupils:	2.4	

The above model is based on a 35 hour or 2,100 minute instructional week including all time within the school day. The provision for regular teachers reimburses the school for the time when these exceptional pupils are mainstreamed into regular classes throughout the school. It costs a school building 2.4 times the cost of an ordinary pupil to provide an equitable educational effort for pupils with this special need. While the school is provided with this allotment, there is flexibility in permitting the school to deviate from the model in practice. If, for example, some pupils would be better served by differing assignments to regular school activities, such can be accomplished providing equivalent instructional objectives are achieved. A major advantage of assigning such classes to school buildings is the anticipation of innovative and unique customized arrangements in keeping with the basic tenet of school site budgeting: the best decisions are made closest to the pupil instructional level. This too is in keeping with the goal of special educational programs, to provide the least restrictive alternatives for each pupil.

An illustration of time and financial support allocations for several types of exceptional classes are illustrated in Figure 7-1. Schools and school districts, using similar analyses may construct a model of locally derived levels of resource allocations for special classes.

Schools tend to welcome the assignment of special classes when appropriate funding accompanies them. Often, the combination of their regular effort and the additional support of special supplementary funds will permit the school to provide full time services of specialists who otherwise might be needed a fractional amount of the time. Also, such students typically spend much of their time in assigned classrooms and may not compete for space or expenses in such school offerings as libraries, musical activities, sports

Figure 7-1

SPECIAL EDUCATION PUPIL WEIGHTINGS

Elementary School

Educable Mentally Retarded	2.3
Emotional Maladjusted	3.7
Learning Disabled	2.4
Learning Disabled Resource	1.65
Trainable Mentally Retarded	3.1
Severely Learning Disabled and Autistic	4.4
Pre-School Language	.4

Junior High School

Educable Mentally Retarded	2.5
Emotional Maladjusted	3.5
Learning Disabled	2.6
Learning Disabled Resource	1.8
Severely Learning Disabled and Autistic	4.7

Senior High School

Educable Mentally Retarded	2.4
Emotional Maladjusted	2.3
Learning Disabled Resource	1.8
Trainable Mentally Retarded	3.1

events, dramatic productions, or general building supply consumption. While such students are expected to participate in such activities according to their abilities and interests, their participation is of,ten at a lesser level of involvement. However, the pollination of exceptional and ordinary pupils is in itself a legitimate objective for each persons' educational growth and development.

Such a special assemblage of funding provisions is not limited to classes for handicapped pupils. A like model could be formulated for pupils who are exceptionally gifted and would be equitably treated by extraordinary funding provisions. Their program might specify additional resources encompassing specialized tutors or lecturers, sophisticated instructional paraphernalia, a broadened selection of intellectual and artistic activities, supplemental trips to stimulating environments, and the ever present requirement of smaller and more specialized pupil/staff ratios. All such costly accouterments need to be factored into a model for funding activities for the support of classes for gifted pupils.

Other specialized funding models could be designed for pupils who attend alternative instructional programs. Where such programs are detached from a school unit, their entire costs must be included in the model. When they are assigned to a school their proportionate expenditure expectations need to be calculated and added to that school appropriation in the form of a weighted per capita allowance for each pupil.

In each model, only atypical costs peculiar to the specific program need be isolated and charted. The mere designation of a specialized group need not indicate a need for additional funding. Often, their specialized activities will supplant other costs. Only the extraordinary additive cost requirements need to be factored into planning models.

Funding Adjustments

Several contemporary school budgeting systems incorporate a provision for looping outcomes and costs. When it is shown that desired outcomes are not achieved, an examination of assigned resources and instructional processing techniques is performed. If

107

the deficiency seems to be the result of inadequate or improper resource assignments, corrections, and adjustments are provided. This integration of costs and benefits enables such procedures to be viewed as a system.

School site budgeting processes are pliable and adaptable to such systematic review processes. Pupils of special education classes customarily have their instructional needs individually prescribed by a mandated team of specialists who formally plan for their placement, their program, and a monitoring of their progress. If as a result of previous planning, expected results are not produced, it is an easy assignment to alter the provisions of the funding model to incorporate different personnel, time, or materials inputs as signalled.

School site budgeting is not a self fulfilling prophecy insofar as funding for exceptional pupil programs is required. Rather than assume a restrictive role on expenditures, it tends to provide a supportive element towards the carrying out of educational decisions. It is ever subject to alteration as conditions warrant. One of school site budgeting's biggest advantages is its ability to chart or map monetary and resource assignments required by nonconformist activities. The precept of all navigation is to establish a fix on current whereabouts. School site budgeting provides the instrumentation for such orientation.

Chapter 8

PERSONNEL CONSIDERATIONS

School site budgeting produces an unusual impersonality in planning for personnel resources. There's a very present danger in handling human elements in a purely statistical manner. The mechanics of school site budgeting provides for the assembly of all members of a job classification into a single group for batch processing. The batch of salaries is totaled and averaged. The resulting average salary is then used as the value or cost for each position of each classification. The reader should be aware that school site budgeting is only a planning process and not an operational accounting system. Therefore the indiscriminate manipulation of positions, using average salaries, does not necessarily reflect the fate of persons or jobholders. Their personal rights, benefits, privileges, working conditions, and survivorship considerations need to be separately recognized. Most often collectively bargained labor agreements will provide the terms and conditions of their job status.

Data Preparation

The first step of personnel planning for school site budgeting requires that a bench mark be established - a uniform foundation from which all planning assumptions will be made. This is done by freezing all payroll lists on a given date at the outset of the budgetary planning cycle. To provide for a reasonable (or sometimes legislatively prescribed) budget planning cycle, the freeze date is about eight months in advance of the start of a fiscal year. For a July 1 - June 30 fiscal year, the freeze date may occur on a pay date in early October, well after the start-up of a new school year and after payroll rosters have been stabilized. On that day in October, a duplicate register of payroll activities is prepared and assembled in a format compatible to the school district's final budgetary presentation format: by programs, by functions, by objects, by services, by grade levels, or any other required dimension. The payroll manifest will serve as a jumping off point to project salaries for the upcoming budget cycle.

The payroll data which have been frozen may serve

a dual purpose. While necessary for budgetary planning, they also will be useful as the basis for collective bargaining positions with labor organizations. Good faith bargaining is enhanced by the use of reliable decoded data uniformly applied and concordant with the figures published as part of the budget planning process. When discussions evolve around the impact of a given action, the basis for measuring the impact may thus be mutually accepted.

Subsequent attritional replacements of school staff members should generally not cause a correction of base level assumptions during the budget planning interval. If attempted, the ever-changing make-up of the base group may contribute to misunderstandings between the bargaining parties or may even promote chicanery within bargaining activities! At a later date it is better to apply a change factor due to the attrition of personnel who were present on the date the payroll registers were frozen. The process of replacing higher salaried retirees with entry level personnel provides a financial gain on each such transaction. Often, the gains through such attrition are reduced by paying the added salary costs of advanced degree attainments during a fiscal year. Other payroll changes are brought about by overtime or extra teaching assignments or by pay reductions for unreimbursed absences. Because of these variabilities, it is recommended that the single frozen salary data base be kept intact and not modified as further budget building activity takes place.

A position count is conducted to ascertain that all authorized positions are presently occupied or represented within the data base and that the number of authorized positions is not exceeded. Next, the lists are adjusted to reflect known transitional positions. If, for example some projects or programs are expiring at the end of the present fiscal year, those positions need to be red-lined. And, if persons presently on leave are expected to return at the start of the upcoming fiscal year, the persons who are presently replacing them need to be replaced by the returnees. The resulting data base should contain all known personnel migrations and reflect the anticipated start-up status of a new fiscal year.

The data base is next massaged to reflect contractually provided wage increments for each eligible employee, to take effect during the next fiscal year. If a multi-year labor agreement is in effect, the total projected salary for each member should be reflected in the planning documents. If future salaries have not yet been determined, the budget builder has the options of estimating subsequent salaries or of placing a funded reserve amount in the basic costs section of the budget. There are advantages to each approach. If the salaries are estimated individually, the resulting average salary rates would be more like the actual costs and benefits assigned to the school building unit budgets. More money is assigned to schools for their planning purposes. But if the estimated salary changes are not assigned to each position and are kept within a reserve account of the basic budget they are less likely to impact on incomplete or concurrent collective bargaining positions.

There is a third alternative to projecting salaries in a lumped reserve or on an individual basis. The projected gross rate of change can be applied to the derived averages of the current salary and benefit costs. An across-the-board percentage would suffice to permit improved school unit planning yet would not necessarily foretell a position of present or future collective bargaining sessions.

The result of either method of projection is an assemblage of best known salaries for all present and migrational personnel, grouped according to salary schedules: teachers, administrators, clerical, service personnel, aides, etc.. Each different salary schedule will produce a different average wage amount. Separate averages are required for like positions that are employed for different time periods. To illustrate, secretarial positions may have a 10.5 or 12 month work year. Each such group requires the calculation of a separate average salary based on their annual service requirement. Schools then have the option of providing funding for school year or calendar year staffing, assuming permissive labor agreements prevail.

If it is expected that any group is to be significantly increased or decreased in membership, the effects of change need to be predicted and accommodated. For example, declining enrollments of pupils may indicate that 15 fewer teaching positions would be required for the upcoming fiscal year. The removal of 15 positions needs to be made prior to the calculation of average salaries. The positions to be cancelled would most likely be the least senior members. Their salaries would be at the lowest end of the salary scale. Thus, their actual (not average) salaries would be removed from the group prior to the determination of the average salary of the remainder of the group. Or, if a significant growth of positions was anticipated, the actual expected salaries would be added to the group prior to the calculation of group average salary. If additional positions were contemplated for a specialized program or project requiring advanced degrees, their salaries may be inordinately high for new employees. Or, if the staff acquisitions are merely to accommodate normal growth or expansion, their salaries may be inordinately low as persons entering the profession for the first time.

When these adjustments have been made to each of the groups of employees, a single salary emerges as the average wage to be paid for each member of the group during the next fiscal year. School building budget planners can add, subtract, trade, barter, or fractionalize the number of each category to be employed in each building. At this point, there need be no regard for actual wages paid to building staff members nor conditions of tenure, seniority, or political entrenchment. This process is merely a budgetary planning simulation experience dealing in average salaries. It is a scheme to reduce all positions to a common denominator for purposes of statistical manipulation. While in the simulation mode, positions have unlimited maneuverability for being assigned to best serve the pupil needs on an equivalent basis - with such decisions being made at the building level, the level where pupil requirements are most obvious!

Employee Benefits

Additional benefit costs for employment of various staff members may approach a full third of wage costs. Insurances and pension costs have a direct monetary requirement and need to be projected for the average wage earner of each group. Some benefits such as paid vacations, holidays, sick leave, and personal business absences may involve a loss of time but have no direct monetary costs except for their replacement with a substitute employee in some instances. Costs due to employee absences can be budgeted as a basic cost or budgeted by individual school units from their building appropriation.

Different salary schedules and their attendant employee benefits will apply to each collective bargaining unit. The average benefit costs need to be separately calculated for each group based on the membership, participation, elective options, and costs of services. Some benefit costs are assessed equally on a position count basis. Others are based on the individual earnings or dependency circumstances of the recipient. It is assumed that each staff member has complete interchangeability of work assignment and that benefits, like salaries, are equally transportable in a planning mode. The average costs of benefits are added to the average costs of salaries for each group of employees and the schools are then provided with the complete average cost for each type of person employed. A sample listing of job categories and average salaries for a school district is shown in Table 4-3.

Schools must always use average rates in making their personnel allocation assignments. They may elect to assign funds to whole or part time positions. Later on, when all school spending decisions have been planned, the central district business office will tally the positions and a net gain or loss of positions will be accumulated. For legislative funding purposes, salaries will be re-established at their actual amounts and entered into the district budget for transmittal to appropriation authorities or processes. Individual schools will have enjoyed manipulative simulation to get the best fit of available funds and staffing requirements without regard to personalities or wages of present personnel. The criteria for staffing is based exclusively on anticipated student program needs.

To assist the schools in planning for personnel services, there should be a wage schedule for part time assignments. For instance, a base work week of 35 hours of active school time might be established on the basis of 5 days of 7 hours each. Such a work day would be all inclusive of lunch, refreshment breaks, planning activities, general pupil supervisory responsibilities, and record keeping requirements. If part time services are to be engaged on an hourly basis, this base period would prevail. An hourly break-down may be essential for the employment of remedial specialists who may be assigned to quarter hour blocks of time in some cases. A different set of assumptions would provide an analysis of teaching periods, where a whole weekly load may be established at 30 periods (including planning). Another means of prorating teaching services may be in terms of whole or half days with each day representing .20 of a full weekly teaching assignment and each morning or afternoon reflecting .10 of a weekly teaching assignment. It is recommended that personnel assignments not be relegated to more than two decimal places or hundredths of a position. While a computer can handle infinite fractionalization, school site budgeting purports to be a process that is readily understood and manageable as a planning device at the school building level. While it is probable that greater accuracy would prevail in dealing with 55 minute instructional periods of a 32 period weekly schedule (.03125), the added complexity seems too great a price to pay. It would be better to round off to .03, a manageable entity.

It is also possible to employ persons for part of a fiscal or school year. A single semester, full time, would be half or .50 of a position that was budgeted for a whole year. Care should be taken in assigning fractional positions to assure that employee benefit escalations need not occur. If it is district policy to provide full fringe benefits to each person working more than 20 hours a week or 50% of a position, the engagement of two such half time employees would cost two whole fringe benefit units. These may be partially offset by having several employees who work less than half a schedule and would receive no added benefits. Their combined jobs would exceed one whole position sans benefits.

The list of average salary rates should contain some hourly rates in order that schools may elect to purchase supplementary services. Such rates should be in accordance with those specified in collectively bargained labor agreements or if the contract does not stipulate hourly wages, they may be calculated by dividing the annual or weekly schedules into hours required. In no case may local schools be granted the autonomy of establishing rates of pay. To do so would cause a proliferation of non-conforming wage rates leading to waste, abuse, and potential misconduct.

A single set of average wage rates must be promulgated and must prevail.

Staffing Guidelines

While schools are given control of funding allocations, they simultaneously need to operate within district policy guidelines. Schools must meet pupil/staff ratios of instructional time requirements (including elective offerings) as prescribed. Often, staff adequacy limits are contained within prevailing labor agreements. Occasionally, custom and neighborhood circumstances dictate some staffing arrangements. Or, some staffing choices are mandated by current management or curricular objectives. A vital part of school site budgeting is the involvement of consumers (parents) in budgetary planning. Their goals may include class size, curriculum content, the engagement and utilization of special subject teachers, and the time schedule under which all of these will operate. Some adjustments to work schedules might best be made at the local building level in order to accommodate lunch and rest periods, planning periods, facility use, and availability of personnel resources.

To achieve a very efficient utilization of personnel, school site budgeting provides the opportunity for split assignments wherein portions of staff salaries and services are assigned to more than one school unit. While such a sharing of staff may appear to be a convenient resolution of a problem, there are added costs associated with the between building travel times that must be subsidized. The time and expense for such commuting is assigned to the basic cost section of the budget since it could not be judiciously assigned to either school. Also problemsome is the time of day when traveling staff members render their services. Most schools follow the maxim of providing the most concentrated instruction during morning sessions when students are more alert and receptive. Yet, a traveling specialist needs some afternoon assignments and must gain them through a compromise of schedule assignments. Occasionally such split assignments cause inequities concerning the inability to schedule school activity assignments in the same manner as stationary staff members.

When staffing decisions are rendered at a building

level, with all school community members having an input to such decisions, a better understanding of staffing trade-offs is likely to occur. If, for example a school must choose between allocating funds to provide for additional staff to relieve teachers for planning or snack break periods or using such funds to continue the employment of a full time regular staff member suffering a borderline decline of student population, a very worldly choice must be made. Or, if some highly specialized elective course offerings do not attract a sufficient clientele, the continuation of that activity needs to be re-examined in terms of assignment of funds to better purposes. Conversely, if new programs are deemed worthy of funding, it becomes necessary to examine all existing programs to determine the weakest link on the survival chain. An inherent levelling process tends to promote gradual changes by accommodation, absorption, integration, and amalgamation. But again, such evolutionary changes are best formulated at the building level by responding to (locally) evident needs.

Replacements for Absentees

There are certain advantages in providing for substitute employees within the basic cost budget section. It can be argued that district-wide leave or absence policies are uncontrollable or inestimable at the building level. It can also be argued that school building leaders can be given the cost incentive of affecting the absence records of staff members. Another choice is to share the cost of replacement (substitute) staff members wherein each building assumes the cost of normal absence expectations and the basic cost section of the budget takes over when long-term (over 7 or 10 consecutive days) absences take place. Schools often have alternates to employing substitutes for absented personnel. Duties may be covered by persons having free time, by combining operations, or by having normally non-teaching administrative staff take over vacated assignments. And, when staff members of buildings realize that their absences may cause a building hardship, they may make a greater effort to report for service. When the cost of replacement personnel is remotely contained within the basic cost budget section there is less awareness at the school building level and correspondingly less motivation for conservation.

116

Basic Cost Budget Personnel

Unlike school building budgeting which deals in average salaries, the basic cost budget section positions are required to be budgeted at actual salaries and benefit costs. They tend to be few in number and highly specialized. They are normally not susceptable to transferrability. There must also be provision for their supportive service costs: travel, in-service activities, dues and fees, and conference expenses.

In some cases, district-wide specialists provided within the basic cost budget section may also take over a minor assignment such as a teaching period within a school. When that takes place, their salary may be split between the basic cost budget section (at actual salary) and the school building budget appropriation (at fractional simulated average teacher salary).

It merits repeating that the goal of school site budgeting is to minimize the basic cost section of the budget and to include everything that is school related in the school unit appropriations.

Other Considerations

The school site budgeting process will accommodate the wholesale re-assignment of staff positions only while dealing in averaged simulated salaries. The recasting of such statistical entities into human form for operational employment purposes may not be so easily accomplished.

A secondary school may elect to employ 5 science teachers in the upcoming budget rather than the 7 currently employed. Decisions of selection may be influenced by labor agreements, district policies or regulations, an examination of each person's credentials, experiences and skills, or perhaps measures of seniority. If another school of the district happens to be simultaneously adding 2 science teachers, the problem becomes one of simple selection for transfer. Or, if normal resignations or attrition dovetails with staff reduction requirements the problem is eased.

When planned staffing changes are to be implemented, localized input will improve the decisions. Local school units may better assess the personalities of persons subject to re-assignment and to fit their psych to the position requirements. Schools must legitimately examine matters of program continuity, curricular thrusts, unmet objectives, or complimentary skills when in the process of changing the assignment of employees.

A final condition to be met is the requirement of labor agreements governing the retention, assignment, or re-deployment of members of the bargaining unit. Labor contracts often contain restrictive conditions concerning management's right to establish, combine, assign, sub-contract, or transfer operations and their attendant personnel. There are also apt to be clauses concerning promotional practices, reduction in force procedures, extra duty assignments of part time personnel, conditions of tenure or certification, and work loads.

Thus, while school site budgeting provides a process for levelling personnel disparities for purposes of planning for school expenditures, there comes a time when operational implementation of school planning decisions must be adjudicated. With or without the use of school site budgeting, changes in the number or nature of position assignments would be problemsome. It seems more orderly to use school site budgeting as a process to focus on the net changes required and then to face the issue of getting the best fit of personnel resources and program requirements.

Chapter 9

PROVIDING THE RIGHT MATERIALS

As earlier indicated, only 2% of a school's financial allocation will ordinarily be available for books, supplies, and instructional materials. All other funds are required for staff and service costs. This relatively small amount, however, becomes very significant when the impact of instructional materials is considered in terms of contributions to the process of teaching. With no materials whatsoever, a learner would gather information only from the spoken word of the teacher, thereby using only one of five available senses. Through careful selection, integrated use, and critical evaluation of instructional materials, teachers can channel information to students simultaneously through all their available sensory probes.

Localized Selection

School site budgeting, in permitting each school to pursue system-wide objectives in its own manner, permits great lattitude in the selection of appropriate teaching and learning aids. Materials tailored to the local instrucational program will improve the effectiveness of the delivery effort. Schools need to consider material selection in light of the personality of the staff members, the style and method of presentation, the scope and sequence of the curriculum, student time on task allocations, the contemporary nature of available resource materials, and the continuous evaluation of products and examination of results. Thus, without regard to logistics, each school building makes the first level decisions regarding the selection and use of appropriate books, materials, and supplies. A form of quality control can be attained by having subject matter specialists (supervisors, coordinators, directors) be familiar with the items being purchased. Their added expertise helps to avoid the acquisition or use of inappropriate materials.

School Purchasing Options

The school instructional program will determine the selection of specialized materials needed to precisely augment the program objectives. Schools may select textbooks and related materials, reference books, work books, periodicals, visual aids, audio-visual materials, maps, globes, charts, models, mock-ups, demonstration apparatus, or any such paraphernalia to best accommodate their instructional syndrome.

Often, teachers will individually engage in spot purchasing to get the exact materials desired. Such transactions may occur at book stores, museums, conventions, shopping centers, or other local businesses. With a ready petty cash reimbursement procedure, the goods are handily gathered and put to use with a minimum of delay and purchase validation.

If several schools utilize the same books or materials a coordinated purchasing effort will produce some volume purchasing economies. Also, schools using parallel instructional programs can trade surplus items for cost saving benefits.

Coordinated purchasing can take place for repititious items that can be identified far in advance of their needed date. For example, magazine subscriptions can be aggregated and bid through a jobber or distributor at a large savings.

A centralized inventory system will promote extended use of purchased materials. While items such as textbooks and work books tend to be dedicated to a single classroom, many of the costly related materials are used only occasionally for demonstration, reinforcement, or enrichment. Maps, globes, charts, filmstrips, audio, video, or data cassettes, computer diskettes, films, models, and demonstration apparatus are easily portable. A very good cost/use ratio can be gained through cooperative sharing of items having occasional use. A data processing facility will provide the required inventory procedure and maintenance of information processes to protect the purchaser's equity and the borrower's accessibility.

It is important that school site budgeting not cause a wasteful redundancy of small volume high cost purchase transactions. Often, laws and regulations which govern school districts contain restrictive purchasing procedures requiring formalized competitive bidding and vendor analysis. If a waiver of such requirements (to accommodate school site decision making) cannot be obtained, it may be possible to split orders into smaller units that do not exceed the maximum purchase limits for formal bidding.

Vendor Relations

In order for schools to be aware of the availability of instructional resource materials, vendor contacts need to be established at the school building level. Such a free interchange should not lead to the abandonment of central purchasing system requirements. The need for verification of funding authorization remains a central business office function. Correspondence regarding shipments, damages, price adjustments, cancellations, tax exemptions, or substitutions must be coordinated by or at least carbon copied to the central business office. There needs to be a distinction made between the school being able to select and acquire the precise product required and orderly business practices required to protect the public interest in providing the products in the least costly and most effective manner. Both goals can be achieved with the school site budgeting process.

Tests of Adequacy

Schools, in allocating funds to all aspects of their domain, need to guard against the tendency to commit too many resources to staff requirements with the danger of having insufficient funds to provide a full range of necessary instructional materials. Since materials, per se, cannot bargain independently or collectively, their advocacy becomes a matter for central district office review. Measures of adequacy include a review of current inventories matched with enrollment projections, an examination of the dates of publication of materials on hand, a look at recent year purchase patterns, and a comparison of per capita expenditure for materials in comparison with other schools of the district. Budget reviewers also need to examine the impact of instructional materials provided by other (nonbudgeted) sources. Donations may be received from parent or civic groups, industrial and commercial sources, and teacher made materials. School leaders need to be especially attentive to materials provided by commercial and industrial trade sources. They need to be critiqued for self-serving bias, intellectual honesty, accuracy, adequacy, promotional advertising, and appropriateness to the instructional program. Passing all these tests, they may be welcomed as a timely supplement of instructional resource materials.

121

Program Accommodations

Individual schools generate a list of books, supplies, and materials, categorized by instructional program. A workable budget form appears as Figures 10-1,2. These allocations will be placed intact in the school district budget, and upon approval of that budget, regular purchasing procedures may begin.

Since budget planning often takes place 8 - 10 months in advance of the fiscal year, there needs to be a provision to alter the budgeting suppositions if circumstances change. Differences may be caused by personnel changes, enrollment variations, alternate or supplemental course offerings, or curriculum revisions. To accommodate such changes, the school site budgeting process provides a transfer date, typically in November or December after all start-up changes are evidenced. On that single occasion, schools are permitted to rearrange accounts for goods and services in order to accommodate changes that could not have been foreseen at budget building time. Since the strength of a budget is its predictive capability, such transfers need to be carefully controlled to protect the integrity of the budget planning process.

Purchasing Considerations

There are economies of scale in purchasing materials in large quantities. Vendors can pass on their savings from order writing, handling, packaging, billing, and shipping expenses. School districts can gain the instructionally tailored advantages of school site budgeting yet the economies of large scale purchasing by separately providing basic school supplies on a centralized basis and by allowing schools to acquire specialized school supplies and materials at the building level. Funding to purchase basic school supplies is provided within the basic (non-site) cost section of the overall district budget. Basic supplies may be centrally warehoused and allocated to the schools on a per capita internal credit voucher basis.

Basic supplies might include all commodities not dedicated to a special instructional program. Basic papers, adhesives, fasteners, writing instruments, color materials, and general supply items are common to all programs and rarely require customized meshing with a curricular offering. Many have a limited shelf life and require stock rotation: carbon papers and ribbons, adhesives, tapes, paints, batteries, copier products, film, and color materials. Such items can be best handled in a commonly inventoried warehouse and dispensed on the basis of first in - first out. Or, for convenient point of use storage in separate school buildings, the same stock rotation plan should prevail.

All non-instructional operational commodities and supplies (floor wax, paper towels, lamps, fertilizer ...) should be centrally purchased and handled.

The major economy of large volume purchasing often comes from packaging methods and shipping charges. If a series of unbroken cartons can be delivered to a single location optimal cost savings will occur. Even where a central warehouse is not maintained, school districts may be able to receive all goods at a common destination and trans-ship to individual buildings at a lower cost. A centralized receiving area also provides more security for incoming merchandise and enables shipping damage claims to be promptly executed. Further savings may be realized if goods are promptly verified and invoices quickly processed for payment. Many vendors offer a 2% discount for payment within 10 days. On large shipments, sizeable sums can be realized from such discounts.

A final advantage of centralized purchasing of basic commodities is the gain from standardization of products. A proliferation of non-standardized items compounds the inventory and warehousing involvement with small quanitities of irregular items. Standardization criteria need to apply to such products as tapes and tape dispensers, staples and staplers, typewriter and office machine ribbons and tapes, calendar pads and holders, printed forms, color match materials, toilet paper and paper towels and their dispensers, cards and files, notebook fillers, floor mops and holders, water color paint pans and paint boxes, and such products for which repair or replacement parts are stocked (pencil sharpeners, flashlights, power cords, etc.).

In summary, school site budgeting purports to establish a better coordination between instructional materials and classroom educational activities.

Specialized materials are attained on a timely basis. Selection decisions are made at a level close to the classroom. Where practicable, savings are realized by large volume purchasing of standardized items and common commodities. The entire process has an element of timeliness that permits quick response to educational program changes. The 2% of funds set aside for the purchase of instructional materials is the second most important aid to learning, second only to the skills of the teaching staff in directing their use.

Chapter 10

SCHOOL DECISIONS

As school building leaders begin the task of developing an expenditure plan for the upcoming fiscal year, they need first to take stock of all the circumstances affecting the present state of the school community.

A review of current staff will reveal strengths and weaknesses, including academic preparation, personal characteristics, professional performance, and overall contributions to the instructional program. A scan of the student population will note the groupings and sizes of classes, their time schedules, the successes achieved, the current needs, and the overall academic and social ambience of the student body. A review of the instructional program should provide an assessment of its adequacy of scope, sequence, timeliness, content, and ability to meet the needs of individual pupils. A review of recent evaluative criteria will aid in defining overall instructional program strengths and weaknesses. Indicative measures can be attained from test results, assessments of student growth and development, scholarship beneficiaries, follow-up studies of graduates, indications of parental satisfaction, and observable student and staff morale. A look at school support staff will provide an estimate of their job performance, adequacy of number, and contribution to support of the instructional program. A review of the physical plant will reveal its ability to accommodate the instructional program, its limitations, and its structural integrity. Finally, a review of the available instructional support materials will provide the building leader with a summary of books, supplies, equipment, and all other essential teaching tools and instructional devices and supportive elements.

Having taken stock of all such components, the school building leader needs to relate those circumstances to present funding support. Would additional money produce different results? What would be the highest priority if additional money became available? What current expenditures should be modified or discontinued? What unmet needs require funding? What operations should be combined (or segregated) for improved effectiveness? What are the major concerns facing this school during the next fiscal year? What two or three management goals should be established? What strategic planning will best help attain those goals? What is the order in which those things might best be accomplished? What obstacles will impair or impede the fulfillment of the goals? If the goals prove to be unattainable, what secondary or tertiary goals could reasonably be achieved?

Armed with this composite analysis of the state of the school, the administrator may examine the packet of budget building materials provided by the central school district and begin to match the above strategies with the resources provided. The administrator must get others, who will participate in the planning process, to develop their own assessment of the status of the school. They too must develop a ranking of the needs of the next fiscal year and the best adoptions to achieve those ends. A deductive reasoning process will enable the school administrator to lead school community members to concensus through participatory planning.

The Budget Planning Packet

In order to develop a school budget, the school is provided with an estimate of the number and types of pupils to be accommodated, a financial allotment and a listing of salary averages for each class of employee. Schools may also be given direction concerning system-wide goals or objectives that require special emphasis in budget planning. Within these resources, schools must plan for providing each student with an equivalent educational opportunity based on the needs of each student. A best accommodation is sought!

Prior to this, the building leader has learned of the items benefitting each school that have been provided for within the basic (non-site) section of the overall school district budget. Those non-instructional, operational, and logistical support activities need not siphon any further funds from the school building appropriations. All assigned funds may be used for local school purposes.

An Opportunity

Budget planning provides a unique opportunity for meaningful participation in school governance by the members of the school community. It is an outstanding communications device, tending to expose for review all aspects of the school enterprise. Opinions are sought in a meaningful, timely, and positive manner. Mutually exclusive thrusts can be matched and compromised. Value judgements require substantiation. Critical selection produces improved judgements.

School site budgeting requires extreme openness and disclosure of all pertinent information regarding the funding of school programs. The costs and benefits of each transaction must stand scrutiny if local based management decisions are to be implemented. Such revelation must of necessity expose weaknesses as well as strengths. Considerable skill is required in acknowledging past failures or shortcomings and providing measures to reduce or prevent their future occurrence. If unsatisfactory results occurred despite the best efforts of an informed group of planners, there is less tendency to damage the confidence in individual leaders. So the process continues, with the school leader freely providing all known components of the planning equation and inviting members of the school community to participate in selecting the conditions and surroundings which will occur in the near future.

School site budgeting tends to extend a concern for budgetary matters throughout the year. Rather than the seasonal cyclical activity peaks of conventional budgeting practices, there is a sustained interest in assessing the results of participatory decisions and the possibility of mid-course corrections by way of fund transfers.

Care must be taken to assure that all group inputs are attained prior to decision making. Decisions must be postponed rather than made early with the hope of ratification. Rubber stamp diplomacy does not satisfy the school site budgetary process requirement of broad based participation in determining school expenditure allocations.

Staff and parent participation might be most effective if some channelling of ideas is promoted. Rather than trying to sort each suggestion from a committee of the whole, a representative committee can screen suggestions and by combination and consensus can expedite the formulation of refined suggestions.

Students may contribute a unique view point in the
process of determining how best to satisfy their educational requirements. Though they have limited maturity, their awareness of daily classroom experience provides a first hand source of information and issue identification. Students will gain new experiences in their
growth continuum by being made aware of the options and
challenges of planning for their instructional programs.
And, receiving a credible explanation of the limitations
on instructional matters due to fiscal resource restrictions, pupils can more understandably cooperate in
finding daily cost-saving or cost-prevention solutions.
While their school program priorities may be different
from adult priorities, they nevertheless require complete examination, value analysis, and a rationalized
response concerning their merits or probabilities of
adoption.

Procedurally, there may be some advantage in
having a professional staff review of budgeting options
prior to input by the laity. An improved planning
process may occur after unworkable or impracticable
positions were defined and discarded and a few refined
options identified for further scrutiny. Staff morale
may be aided by having such an alternative selection
planning process take place first within that body.
Keen staff interest will be accorded to a review of
spending options which will directly affect their
future. Budgetary decisions cope with options of job
assignment and transfer, matters of creating or eliminating positions, specific academic or extra-curricular
duty assignments, and conditions of employment.

Another branch of the school community concerned
with budgetary and program planning is the interested
parent and neighborhood group. The school building
leader must exercise skill in obtaining genuine input
from such people while simultaneously setting parameters
to their influence. The school leader's role is to
attain concensus consistent with the leader's professional assessment of the best course of action available
While parent opinion polls, questionnaires, conferences,
study groups, research findings, or directive petititons
are all important influences on school destiny decisions
the professional judgement of the school leadership must
be the final determinant.

Parental (and community) participation will best

take place within a series of directional guidelines. The limits of exploration and recommendation can be prescribed by skillfully describing the tasks or questions that need to be addressed. This will indicate what is supposed to be accomplished and by inference might indicate concerns that are being addressed by others. To obtain this atmosphere, parents should be provided with a statement of circumstances and a set of questions to be addressed. The purpose of such structure is to channel parental resources constructively while avoiding wasteful excursions into unadjustable legal, academic, professional, or otherwise irresolute matters.

School site budgeting requires an examination of the provision of equivalent educational offerings for students. The process protects the rights and interests of the students from the intrinsic demands of adult pressure groups. Resources are equally available to all student needs. Student welfare decisions are rationalized, not compromised. In all of this, there will be an accumulation of local influences on school programs. Each school will be in a position to plan according to locally perceived needs concerning matters of ethnics and culture, economic strata, sociological concerns, academic ambitions, and neighborhood customs. Secondary schools must additionally consider all the in-house competing viewpoints when parcelling funds. How can the school best determine the proportionate allocations to acadamia, sports, career and vocational interests, extra-curricular activities, the arts, the sciences, and the social development of the students?

The school site budgetary process literally brings individuality to each school unit, consistent with the basic assumptions that the best decisions are made closest to the arena where they are to be carried out. This budgetary (and program) planning process embroils parents in a healthful examination of their local school surroundings and the complex choices of satisfying infinite aspirations with finite resources. They will gain an awareness of the constructive efforts of school professionals engaged in designing instructional programs to best serve each student. Parents gather background information regarding school matters and are thus better able to empathize when school issues require public understanding and support.

Limiting Options

The fixed element of school site budgeting is the nature and size of the student population. All budgetary decisions are designed to suit <u>student</u> needs! One of the first of such decisions is the matter of student grouping for instructional purposes. Tentative schedules need to be arranged to plot sizes of classes, numbers of classes, nature of classes, time schedules, and a display of options or variations for each.

For example, an elementary school might be informed that enrollment for grade 3 is estimated to be 56 students during the next school year. The class size choices might be 2 of 28, 2 of 19 and 1 of 18, 4 of 14, or 3 morning sessions of 18:19 and 2 afternoon sessions of 28. Other choices would involve a review of the grades above and below (4th and 2nd) to examine the possibility of combining into a split-grade combination class. Still another option is to plan for extra paraprofessional assistance if any class size appear to be overly enlarged. In examining these options the building leader must analyze the prevailing local circumstances including staff availability and their potential for accommodating each arrangement, the precise characteristics of the students involved, the historical treatment of this group of students, the availability of classrooms to house the various options, and perhaps lastly, the relative costs and benefits of each configuration.

While planning for pupil-class arrangements within secondary schools all of the above decision factors are further compounded by schedule restrictions and the degree of elective offerings provided within inflexible time constraints. But in each case, there are options that may be elected. The job of the school building leader is to assist in developing and isolating such issues for full and impartial examination. Many choices will directly affect the employment and working conditions of staff members and therefore require great skill in their delicate handling and debate. Having averaged all salaries for planning purposes, schools are not dealing with personalities when plotting future staffing options. The process assumes that staff transfers can be achieved in the interest of getting the best configurations for student success.

Since 98% of local school expenditures are required for personnel assignments, the matter of alternative budget planning swirls around staffing decisions.
The views of current staff members, parents, the neighborhood, and students need to be evaluated in seeking
the best budgetary solution. It is recommended that
each building provide a formal statement describing the
process by which alternatives were developed, reviewed,
and critically selected by each group of constituents.

After completing the staffing decisions, there must
be a reasonable sum of money available for allocation
to books, materials, supplies, and other resources.
Again, there would be opportunity for widespread review
and rational contributions from the local school budget
planners.

Selecting Options

The school building leader should not finalize
budgetary decisions until expert support staff opinion
has been gathered. While local building choices are
acceptable, it would be prudent to seek the counsel of
subject matter specialists insofar as curriculum decisions are concerned. A review of district-wide objectives needs to be matched with local school expenditure planning decisions. The means of achieving the
objectives is a local option. The de facto achievement
of district-wide objectives is a central mandate. Therefore, budgetary planning decisions must be sold to a
central review authority, typically the superintendent
of schools or the superintendent's delegated administrator.

Schools should produce a few local objectives at
the outset of the budget planning process. There may
be some perceived shortcomings that need to be attacked.
Or there may be program improvements that beg for implementation. Perhaps some customary practices have
outlived their usefullness. Or perhaps minor shifting
of emphases will produce a vastly improved student
instructional climate. The budget acts as a vehicle
to identify and modify any such local objectives.
Schools gain considerable control of their destiny
within the school site budgeting process.

While scrutinizing local school operations, the
budget planners may be faced with some "make or buy"

choices. The selection of a new textbook series may be contrasted with the likelihood of teacher-made instructional materials, each of which may have obvious advantages. Or, decisions regarding the role of paraprofessionals vis a vis the availability of parent and community volunteers. Schools may also examine tuition payments to other schools for special instructional services for their exceptional students. Rather than spending the money in that fashion, schools may elect to provide local programs of equivalent nature. Another avenue for exploration is the examination of instructional time expenditures. Schools may improve their time on task ratios by deliberate planning to achieve that end. This would include a review of the time and costs for field trips, assembly programs, and interscholastic competitions that siphon instructional moments.

One criticism of the school site budgetary process is its tendency to preserve the present state of affairs of the school. If all available resources are assigned in a manner designed to perpetuate the present circumstances, no funds would be available for program growth or improvement. One method of funding of program improvements would be to set aside an amount of money immediately upon receipt of the schools' allocation. Such a research and development fund can subsequently be doled out through a process of competitive examination of expenditure proposals. Another way to fund for program improvement is to critique extant programs with a view towards supplanting them if their contributions are exceeded by their costs. A third approach would be that of insisting that some program improvement be provided in each discipline. Such improvements may not all be of substantial dimensions, but the positive thrust of seeking such growth is a valued result. Finally, it would be possible to set aside a sum of money within the basic costs section of the overall district budget in order to fund program improvement efforts on a grant-like basis. Whichever funding method is chosen, the matter of making school programs better is an ongoing management goal. Without an element of improvement, external evolutionary progress would by-pass a stagnating school program thereby rendering it ineffectual.

When it appears that the school's comprehensive budget plan has been completed, a self-examination of the product would be in order. Indicators of sound budgeting theory should be reviewed. A well conceived budget is a strategic planning device, incorporating the objectives the school wished to achieve, a review of alternate ways of achieving those ends, and a built-in yardstick to measure accomplishments. The strategic outcomes are best met by a series of tactical activities.

A degree of situation analysis is required. Planners need to define opportunities and the potential for breaking with tradition. Planners need to define threats, things that may work to retard or impede a well formulated budget plan. And, planners need to define critical issues that can and should be addressed as potential influencers of future events. In many cases the intuitive insight of the school building leader is tested by budget building events.

After screening the budget for omissions or oversights, the building leader may apply several comparative techniques to corroborate the school budget plan. One relevant measure is the relationship of fixed costs, variable costs, and mixed costs. Another enlightening statistic would be compilation of direct labor costs and indirect labor costs. Some analysts use measures of controllable costs and non-controllable costs. The building leader needs to produce assumptions of cost assignments. Such assumptions may in reality be little more than a guess. The techniques of analyzing school budgets must rely on inferential measures since the handy "return on investment" ratio of commercial enterprises is not germaine to a nonprofit or service institution.

Since schooling is a progressive process, there needs to be a linear review of the schools' productive role. Insights can be gained from showing relationships of certain cost elements on a multi-year basis. Some useful categorical measures available to school building leaders are listed here. By developing some such measures as percentages of overall statistical populations and showing the ratios or proportional relationships, the school budget readers can be provided with an informed perspective.

administration/all expenditures
consumer price index/all expenditures
costs/per capita

energy costs/all expenditures
enrollment/all expenditures
fixed costs/total costs
instructional costs/non-instructional costs
library services/circulation volume
local support/state, federal support
maintenance costs/property value
mandated costs/school expenditures
median salaries/annual change or inter-group comparisons
professional salaries/all salaries
remedial services/all expenditures
resources/per capita
special education services/all expenditures
sports programs/all expenditures or per capita
staff/enrollment
staff costs/material costs
time on tasks/available time
transportation mileage/enrollment or passengers
utilities/all expenditures
wages/benefits

To test the reasonableness of any such data, a building
leader may obtain comparative data from similar schools
or can develop a yardstick of a group of schools and
plot the school's relative position on the assembled
scale. That measure is especially valuable on a longi-
tudinal basis that would expose any trends in expenditure patterns within that group of schools.

Compiling and Reviewing

When all budget planning decisions are made, the
school building leader completes a form for transmittal
to the central district office, (see Figures 10-1,2).
The entire local school community should be made aware
of the final judgements at the building level. While
hopefully all concerns have been resolved, there is a
chance for local decisions to be appealed to higher
authority. Since this budget is yet in the planning
stages, changes are more readily accomplished than
during the implementation stage. However, central administrators must be reluctant to substitute their
judgement for that of the persons closest to the arena.
The central reviewer needs to be concerned with strategic matters while leaving the tactical choices to the
local building leaders.

STAFFING

(SCHOOL)

(ENROLLMENT)

GRADE	STUDENTS	TEACHERS
K		( )
1		( )
2		( )
3		( )
4		( )
5		( )
6		( )
SP. ED. RESOURCE		( )
SP. ED. IIITENSIVE		( )
ART		( )
READING		( )
HEALTH/PHYS. ED.		( )
MUSIC		( )
SPEECH/HEARING		( )
GIFTED		( )
LIBRARIAN		( )
TOTAL		( )

@ $22.314

PRINCIPAL	( )	X $32,633
PSYCHOLOGIST	( )	X $27,917
SECRETARY	( )	X $10,811
AIDE	( )	X $ 7,413
HEAD CUSTODIAN	( )	X $15,364
CUSTODIAN	( )	X $13,087
TEACHER SUBSTITUTES		DAYS @ $30.00
CLERICAL SUBSTITUTES		DAYS @ $27.00
AIDE SUBSTITUTES		DAYS @ $22.00
TUTORING		HRS. @ $ 9.75
LUNCH AIDE		HRS. @ $ 3.37

STAFF TOTAL $ _____

N.B. SHOW PRESENT YEAR DATA IN PARENTHESES.

FIGURE 10-1

135

ELEMENTARY SCHOOL

	BOOKS & MATERIALS	SUPPLIES	EQUIPMENT
OFFICE	[ ]	[ ]	[ ]
GENERAL	[ ]	[ ]	[ ]
KINDERGARTE.	[ ]	[ ]	[ ]
ART	[ ]	[ ]	[ ]
READING	[ ]	[ ]	[ ]
HEALTH/ P.E.	[ ]	[ ]	[ ]
MATH	[ ]	[ ]	[ ]
MUSIC	[ ]	[ ]	[ ]
SCIENCE	[ ]	[ ]	[ ]
ENGLISH	[ ]	[ ]	[ ]
SOCIAL STUDIES	[ ]	[ ]	[ ]
LIBRARY	[ ]	[ ]	[ ]
TESTING	[ ]	[ ]	[ ]
CAREER ED.	[ ]	[ ]	[ ]
SPECIAL ED.	[ ]	[ ]	[ ]

COPYING   [   ]
PROFESSIONAL BOOKS   [   ]
DUES & FEES   [   ]
TEXT REBINDING   [   ]
TEXT REPLACEMENT   [   ]
CONFER./MEETINGS   [   ]
TRAVEL REIMB.   [   ]
EXTRA CURR. TRANSP.   [   ]
STUDENT ACTIVITIES   [   ]

TOTAL OTHER EXPENSES $ _____

GRAND TOTAL (_____) _____
            PREVIOUS   THIS
            YEAR   YEAR

FIGURE 10.1

136

STAFFING

(SCHOOL)				
( ) (ENROLLMENT)				

			STAFFING		
ALTERNATIVE EDUCATION	[ ]		PRINCIPAL, H.S.	( )	X 38,116
ART	[ ]		PRINCIPAL, JR. HI. SCH.	( )	X 37,800
BUSINESS EDUCATION	[ ]		ASST. PRINCIPAL	( )	X 35,395
ENGLISH	[ ]		SYCHOLOGIST	( )	X 27,917
FOREIGN LANGUAGE	[ ]		WORK/STUDY COUNSELOR	( )	X 28,867
GUIDANCE COUNSELORS	[ ]		ACTIVITIES COORDINATOR	( )	X 22,948
HEALTH/PHYS. ED.	[ ]		SECRETARY (12 MONTH)	( )	X 13,843
HOME ECONOMICS	[ ]		SECRETARY (10.5 MONTH)	( )	X 10,811
INDUSTRIAL ARTS	[ ]		AIDE	( )	X 7,413
MATH	[ ]		HEAD CUSTODIAN	( )	X 17,534
MUSIC	[ ]		CUSTODIAN	( )	X 13,087
READING	[ ]		TEACHER SUBSTITUTES	___ DAYS	@ 30.00
SCIENCE	[ ]		CLERICAL SUBSTITUTES	___ DAYS	@ 27.00
SOCIAL STUDIES	[ ]		AIDE SUBSTITUTES	___ DAYS	@ 22.00
SPEC. ED. RESOURCE	[ ]		TUTORS	___ HOURS	@ 9.75
SPEC. ED. INTENSIVE	[ ]		STUDENT AIDES	___ HOURS	@ 3.37
LIBRARIAN	[ ]				
SPEECH/HEARING	[ ]				
GIFTED	[ ]				
CAREER SPECIALIST	[ ]				
TOTAL ( )	@ $22,314			STAFF TOTAL $ _____	

N.B. SHOW PRESENT YEAR DATA IN PARENTHESES.

FIGURE 10-2

(SECONDARY SCHOOL)

	BOOKS & MATERIALS	SUPPLIES	EQUIPMENT	
ART	[ ]	[ ]	[ ]	TEXT REBINDING [ ]
BUSINESS ED.	[ ]	[ ]	[ ]	TEXT REPLACEMENT [ ]
READING	[ ]	[ ]	[ ]	COPYING [ ]
ENGLISH	[ ]	[ ]	[ ]	PROFESSIONAL BOOKS [ ]
FOREIGN LANGUAGE	[ ]	[ ]	[ ]	DUES & FEES [ ]
HEALTH/PHYS. ED.	[ ]	[ ]	[ ]	COMMENCEMENT EXPENSES [ ]
HOME ECONOMICS	[ ]	[ ]	[ ]	COMPUTER SERVICES [ ]
INDUSTRIAL ARTS	[ ]	[ ]	[ ]	CONF./STAFF DEVELOP. [ ]
MATH	[ ]	[ ]	[ ]	ALT. ED. SVCS. COSTS [ ]
MUSIC	[ ]	[ ]	[ ]	EXTRA CURR. SALARIES [ ]
SCIENCE	[ ]	[ ]	[ ]	SPORTS COSTS [ ]
SOCIAL STUDIES	[ ]	[ ]	[ ]	INTRAMURAL COSTS [ ]
ALTERNATIVE ED.	[ ]	[ ]	[ ]	DRAMA COSTS [ ]
LIBRARY	[ ]	[ ]	[ ]	MUSICAL PROD. COSTS [ ]
PSYCHOLOGICAL	[ ]	[ ]	[ ]	GIFTED SERVICES [ ]
SPEC. EDUCATION	[ ]	[ ]	[ ]	EXTRA CURR. TRANSP. [ ]
CAREER ED.	[ ]	[ ]	[ ]	
WORK STUDY	[ ]	[ ]	[ ]	
OFFICE	[ ]	[ ]	[ ]	
GENERAL	[ ]	[ ]	[ ]	

TOTAL EXPENSES $ _____

GRAND TOTAL [PREVIOUS YEAR _____ THIS YEAR _____]

FIGURE 10-2

138

Thus, the central administrative reviewer provides each school with an in-depth interview to confirm the thoroughness of their budget planning elections. Primarily, the focus is on the potential for achieving district-wide objectives with the plan presented. The central reviewer must also verify compliance with district policies and regulations, conformity to the provisions of collectively bargained labor agreements, and the satisfaction of all legal and procedural mandates.

The central review authority, having confirmed the judgements made at the building level, forwards the building budgets to the next level for review; the central district authority. At this time the school budgets may also be compiled in the conventional budget format for district-wide review by function-object, program, line-item, activity, or other prescribed form.

It can be shown that hundreds or thousands of people have had an input in planning for next year's operation of a school system and that the decisions affecting each student were made in the environs where the student functions.

The central review authority is provided with an executive summary of each school's operational proposals and is able to examine their aptitude for contributing to the system-wide goals of the school district. Further review can disclose proposed changes designed to improve student achievement and changes to improve operational effectiveness.

Armed with all such information, the central review authority can substantiate the proposals to the final fund appropriating source.

Summarizing the schools' role in the school site budgeting process requires a review of the technical, managerial, political, judicious, and perceptive skills of the school building leader. That person is provided with a sum of money, an estimate of clientelle, a series of wage rates, and a set of goals and objectives that must be achieved. The intent is to get satisfaction of student needs from available resources. This is to be achieved while working within the prescribed rules, regulations, laws, policies, labor agreements, and local customs.

There are three major phases of the building level budget planning process:

1. A detailed review of present circumstances.
2. Identification of needs.
3. The assignment of anticipated resources.

The leader must provide an atmosphere wherein staff members may participate in planning for their future contributions to the instruction of students. Parents and community members must also be accorded the opportunity of helping to shape the school's immediate outlook. Spending (and program) decisions emerge from a grinding process where proposals are fed into the school governing publics and refined decisions emerge via the skillful negotiation of the building administrator. The common denominator for all such decisions is student welfare. The special needs of each student require individual identification and corresponding satisfaction.

A high degree of acceptance of such decisions is required of all participants in order to assure their maximum contributions for successful accomplishment of planned programs. Judgements must be balanced so that personnel and material expenditures are equally provided for. Schools must be encouraged to exceed the status quo by providing program improvement options.

Finally, the school budget is assembled and forwarded to higher authority for review, confirmation, and integration into the district budget.

Chapter 11

QUALITY CONTROL

An industrial manufacturing process can achieve a high level of quality control by regulating the raw materials, fabrication, assembly, and finishing of a product. An endless stream of identical items may be produced. Each unit produced may be precisely measured and its quality compared to each other unit, with virtually no variance.

A schooling process cannot be so readily homogenized and evaluated. Assume that it were possible to control the raw materials (such as with identical twins), the presentation of information, and the provisions of enrichment experiences. Student assimilation would vary by complex processes of discovery, perception, sythesis, motivation, and retention. Further complicating the issue is the lack of agreement concerning the the body of knowledge to be mastered. Add the dimensions of multi-plant locations and interlocking directorships, and the formidable problems of educational process evaluation become apparent.

In evaluating the results of an educational enterprise, it is necessary to look both at the product and the process used to achieve the results. There are many ways of measuring the ingredients and methodology of instruction. They respond to measures of time, space, materials, staffing ratios, pupil classifications, professional skills inventory, program content, and other present characteristics. The far more difficult assessment involves looking into the minds and bodies of students to determine how they have been affected by all the things they have experienced under the guise of education. We must quickly admit that a student spends little more than 10% of all time in a school situation, or about 15% of waking hours. To discriminate between in-school and out of school learning accomplishments is not a likely act in view of the widespread availability of books, magazines, newspapers, television, and microcomputers. This chapter was not designed to respond to the overall challenge of educational evaluation. It is intended to provide some insight into the peculiar requirements of monitoring the quality of instruction within the splintered administrative structure of school site budgeting. In decentralizing school management and program planning, there is added concern that the results must be in accordance with a single quality standard: district-wide goals and objectives. Each building has a high degree of autonomy in designing means to achieve similar ends. But, achieve they must!

Questions of student achievement are most frequently asked when school budgets are presented to the central office review authority. That also happens to be the time when they are most handily related to input expectations. While a precise match of input-output is not apparent when dealing with human achievement, it can be shown that results can be affected by focused efforts. When a learning deficiency is identified and isolated, it can be aided by individually prescribed activity.

Centrally provided management decisions must be specific enough to satisfy the majority of clientelle and flexible enough to accommodate the peculiar needs of those who deviate from the average. Decentralized (school based) management can deal with smaller populations and produce educational program decisions that are more specifically tailored to the requirements of each learner. This is the greatest advantage of school site budgeting - to make customized decisions concerning the best instructional program for each student!!

Time On Task

In reviewing school building budgets, one of the handiest measures of instructional offering is an analysis of time devoted to each activity. Where laws and policies prescribe the (often minimal) amount of instructional time required for each subject, there may be little room for negotiation. However, school building leaders can overcome restrictive mandates of time by providing enlightened interdisciplinary approaches to instruction. It being impossible to remove reading and writing skills from any subject, the unlikely concept of mandated rigid time blocks becomes apparent. But as a place of beginning, a school budget should enable the reviewer to estimate the amount of time intended for each instructional activity. If schools vary considerably in their time allocations for varying purposes, the central review authority should examine the reasons underlying the discrepancies. It is not unlikely that some district objectives may specify the time requirements for some instructional activities. Adherence to those requirements needs to be verified. Other temporal requirements may be contained in labor agreements specifying the conditions of employment.

In elementary schools, elements of student fatigue need to be considered when reviewing instructional time schedules. The morning hours provide the greatest opportunity to provide conceptual or abstract reasoning activities. Instruction in reading, mathematics, and language are normally assigned to morning slots, while physical education, music and arts are typically relegated to afternoon periods. While not universally scheduled in that fashion, the broad concept of morning alertness is often applied. This scheduling concept may be somewhat affected by the school site budgetary process. The process enables schools to purchase part time professional instruction. If part time assistance is to be budgeted for the "morning" subjects, the travelling specialist would only be retained for half a day. Generally, labor agreements would protect the job rights of members of the bargaining unit and would strive to obtain contract language that would require full time teaching assignments wherever feasible. In order to employ the roving staff members on a full time basis, there needs to be some shifting of instructional time blocks or they may receive off-peak assignment to instructionally related (or remedial) duties. In secondary schools the rotational daily schedule of the more challenging learning experiences is an accepted practice. Secondary school schedule problems are more apt to be complicated by space and staff availability, the requirement for double periods for some activities, and the scheduling of extracurricular activities. The central office review authority may compare proposed time assignments with those of prior years in order to quickly spot deviations requiring explanation (see Table 10-2). There is little disagreement that the amount of time assigned to an instructional activity is a key element affecting the attained outcomes. Further measures might be made of the time sequencing within each instructional offering. A graded and logical progression of new experiences will enhance the probabilities of successful instruction taking place.

Student Groupings

The second factor to be reviewed when evaluating school site budget propositions is the manner in which pupils are assembled for instructional purposes. Though there is no accepted standard for a pupil-teacher ratio, some studies have indicated that interactions between pupils and teachers are grossly affected by varying their numeric relationship. Larger classes in general provide more lecturing by teachers whereas smaller classes in general provide for increased personal interaction and educational discovery. There is some evidence that some students are more educationally productive in small classes while others gain more from the wider range of resources, knowledge, and other skills contributed by members of a large group. Often, group size and configurations are set in response to district objectives. Where that is the case, the school site budget may be evaluated in one measure by the degree to which it achieves the prescribed relationships. Where class sizes or teaching loads are specified in labor agreements there should still be an ongoing evaluation of the outcomes from such requirements. A labor agreement generally covers a period of one to three years, subject to renegotiation. Where it can be demonstrated that restrictive staffing clauses have a significant influence on realized learning outcomes, either party to the agreement may propose appropriate modifications for collective bargaining.

Standardized Tests

Pupil achievement scores from standardized testing programs constitute another evaluative measure of the schools' instructional effectiveness. Care must be taken in drawing universal conclusions from such a single faceted measure. Standardized tests show a student's relative position within a scoring distribution. To better assess the results of schooling, standardized scores and standard deviations are established for a grade level and results are compared to the position of comparable students. Over a period of time, the assembly of such data may permit some inferential evaluation of a school's influence on students. But caution should dictate that results may be affected by the innate variance (smartness) in the groups of students selected for comparison. It is not unknown for significant differences in the collective attributes of grade groupings from year to year. Also, the data may be affected by the maturity level or grade groupings of students that experience normal growth at a varied pace.

Nevertheless, standardized achievement scores enable a skilled observer to make growth comparisons between and among local schools and schools outside of the district. Gross changes in educational input or processes are likely to be flagged.

Criterion-Referenced Tests

A better measure of a school's output can be attained through the development of a series of tests that will indicate the degree to which students have attained prescribed skills and understandings and subject matter mastery. Such tests show student progress towards the accomplishment of earlier agreed specific objectives. The objectives are stated in measurable terms and standards or criteria of performance, thus: criterion-referenced. Standards may be expressed as a percentage of attainment which may be finitely measured, observed, deduced, or implied. The process is especially useful for comparing two or more different approaches towards achieving similar results. Judgements of "better" techniques and processes are more judiciously inferred.

Subject matter competencies that are to be measured may be obtained in several ways. Publishers have assembled sets of universally acceptable criteria which school districts may purchase, edit, purge, refine, and adopt as instructional goals. Or, criteria may be established through teacher-prepared locally developed items. In either case, local teachers must ratify the test objectives if they are to be used as a measure of pupil progress.

A third source of criterion-referenced objectives would be from item banks or exchanges operated by regional educational associations or universities. As usual, care must be taken to assure that their selection and adoption satisfies local staff and community expectations.

Criterion need to be specifically stated so that their accomplishment can be realized. Yet, they should not be so narrow or restrictive to encourage singular teaching efforts to the exclusion of instructional enrichment activities. A test may only determine what has been achieved (at the time of the test) and what has yet to be achieved. The diagnosed results indicate the unmet needs of students. Care must be taken to avoid the pitfalls of using tests as a dominant director of school programs or student well-being. The competency based testing movement poses a danger of compressing instructional training into tight channels of study, perhaps at the expense of a comprehensive educational experience. Criterion-reference testing, as constructed, provides many advantages in promoting an educational program that is both intense and comprehensive. Criterion-reference testing lends itself particularly well to school site budgeting wherein instructional options are available at each building level. Programs designed for individual student needs demand assessment on an individualized basis, per item, and per objective. Conversely, lock-step instruction would not require an appraisal of individual performance since the program design would not accommodate individual needs. In that case, age-group norms would be a better evaluative criteria to measure batch processing efforts.

Determining Objectives

What is it that schools are trying to accomplish? In response to such a question, school districts need a series of specific objectives that would serve to pilot the programs, guide the staff, inform the public, and provide a series of measures by which student changes might be measured. To achieve these purposes, the objectives should be stated in terms of learner outcomes, things that students should gain as a result of experiencing the activities.

Each course of study requires a well reasoned set of specific objectives. Each objective should contain its own measure of accomplishment in order that participants (teachers, students, administrators, and parents) may know what is expected of them. They provide a yardstick for the definition of success. Objectives need to be tightly prescribed so the learner will know precisely what is expected and the conditions that are to prevail while engaged in the activity. A common set of objectives would have applicability throughout the school district. While each building

is permitted to pursue instruction in a locally determined fashion, the single set of objectives are the
criteria by which instructional progress is to be evaluated.

A single year's performance is a very slim data
base on which to draw inference of a school's instructional effects. But, a multi-year accumulation of data
provides a more meaningful indication of instructional
production. Typically, the common set of instructional
objectives do not vary substantially from year to year.
Minor changes may be made to accommodate a differing
curricular emphasis, and a certain amount of topical
updating may occur. But the essence of preparing a
set of instructional objectives is the test of well
conceived and lasting attributes. The objectives should
strive for a balance so that specific knowledge and comprehension of a subject is accompanied by indicators of
problem solving ability and attitudinal and behavioral
changes. The overly simplified cognitive-affective .
approach to instructional outcomes are more often amalgamated with considerable overlapping taking place.

The program objectives not only serve as a chart
of production and accomplishment, they double as an
outstanding communicative device for illuminating the
schools' programs for public awareness and understanding. While not all students will progress at the same
rate or achieve the same levels of fulfillment, the
students and parents will better understand their personal status on the continuum. They will also be made
aware of intentions or requirements for progression
to unachieved objectives. A well defined and posted
series of expectations removes the innuendo of pupil
teacher favoritism or ill-defined subjective measures.

Other Measures

While criterion-referenced testing provides the
major source of comparison by and between school
buildings, there are other indicators of school performance that contribute some worthwhile information.
Follow-up studies of graduates may provide a valuable
critique of a school's production. Care must be taken
to treat the bias of the responders if responses are
only obtained from a fraction of the population.

A review of pupil honors and failures lists provide some information regarding the grading practices

147

employed in a school. A review of teacher grade distribution data will illustrate individual teacher attitudes towards the measurement of pupil achievement. Often, grading practices must be enlightened prior to the implementation of criterion-referenced objective evaluation.

A casual review of statistical information regarding the pupil population can provide inferential measures of school quality by examining attendance records, grade retentions, accelerated promotions, drop outs, and disciplinary suspensions.

Opinion polls are often highly developed and commercially attainable. If rendered to parents, staff, and pupils, the agreement and/or variance with school matters can be gleaned. As with any pool of opinions, sensitive treatment of conclusions requires an in-depth and sometimes follow-up study of root statements.

The Composite Evaluation

This chapter has illustrated the many techniques available to review the performance of single school buildings when left to their own selection of instructional inputs and processes. There are observable characteristics of staff adequacies, time allocations, materials expenditures, and student personnel data. The standardized test score data are available as a measure of grade level performance. The development and adoption of a set of program objectives and measures of their fulfillment is the single most valuable indicator of each school's satisfaction of the needs of each pupil. The reason for adopting a school site budgeting process is to do a better job of providing individual and equivalent educational programs for all students. Without an ongoing evaluation, the quality of each school's program would be suspect at worse or unequal at best.

Chapter 12

GETTING STARTED

When a school district wants to adopt a school site budgeting process, the first question to be addressed is: WHY? Unless the response is a loud and clear declaration of a desire to deliver equivalent and suitable educational opportunities to each child, the district could better expend its managerial resources in other directions. School site budgeting offers no other promise. In providing for the individual needs of pupils, this budgeting process spins off several highly desirable by-products. First, there is the advantage of enabling scores of people to be immersed in the planning for improved school services. Secondly, there's the element of self-determination that provokes positive attitudes towards school operations. Thirdly, there is the development of a highly ordered set of instructional objectives and a detailed accounting of the allocation of resources. But these several advantages could be achieved by re-orienting almost any existing budgetary planning process. Only the school site budgeting process encompasses them in totality as truly essential to the success of the venture. So the first step towards adoption requires that the policy makers of the school district come to grips with the overriding concepts of student individuality and equality.

Policy Makers

The key concept that needs resolution at a policy making level is the question of decentralizing the control of the school district. It can be disconcerting to break up and parcel out the decision making and accountability practices formerly reserved to a central administrative locus. With decentralization, the spectre of redundancy and uneven progress needs to be acknowledged. The ready access to system-wide information is apt to be altered. A new degree of confidence is to be placed with many formerly subordinate administrators. There must be tolerance of multi-faceted responses to common events within the district. In short, policy makers need to be conditioned for the major shifting of emphases from a single source (the superintendent) to multiple cost centers. Just as there is no such thing as being a little bit pregnant, there's no conceptual scheme for successfully adopting a portion of the school site budgeting process. It requires the total commitment of the policy making authority of a school district. Staffing decisions that may have been centrally made as matter of policy, suddenly are generated by school building leaders as a matter of planning within the agreed resource assignments. The policy makers are cast in the role of examining and supporting the broad based decisions of the staff and school constituency.

If after examining the pros and cons of school site budgeting the policy makers wish to adopt such a process, a simple resolution to that affect will direct the chief administrative officer to implement the decision with all deliberate speed. Prior to that decision, however, it is assumed that the workings of the school site budgeting process were thoroughly aired in public and the policy makers were representative of the community in their leadership assumptions.

Chief Administrative Officer

Here, too, it is required that total commitment to the concept of school site budgeting be clearly defined as the way to provide equivalent and individualized instruction to each student. Nothing short of that commitment will enable the process to succeed. The chief administartive officer is most singularly affected by relinquishing much decision making to subordinate administrators. In accepting that premise, the chief administrator is immediately faced with the problem of scripting the changeover and most importantly in preparing the building level administrators for their new responsibilities in making critical planning decisions and recommendations.

The chief administrator needs to formulate a time line indicating reasonable targets for each phase of implementation. The start of the fiscal year of the district is the logical time for changing the budget planning process. It is likely that a smoother transition will occur if ample time has been provided in the current fiscal year to synthesize the entire school site budgeting process as a parallel exercise to the in-place budget.

More basic, however, is the need for training staff members in the intricasies of school site budgeting requirements. Unlike other recent budget planning systems (program based, zero based, exception based) there is not a requirement for the generation of extensive philosophical documentation. The only pre- paratory documentation is the design of forms and pro- cedures, mostly accomplished by the school district business office. Later, there will be a need for polishing the district-wide goals and objectives, particularly when budget reviewers want to match resource assignments to anticipated outcomes. But that's probably not very different from the in-place budget plan review sequence.

The chief administrative officer is still the architect for the plotting of the school district. As such, the planning for handling special local options must take place at that level. Judgements are needed in order to establish what budgetary entities are to be centrally retained in the basic costs section and which elements are to be relegated to schools for building level planning. (The more the better - to schools). There are also some central decisions required con- cerning the handling of quasi-building functions such as alternative learning environments or extremely specialized programs for exceptional students. Whether they can best be planned centrally or building-wise requires determination. A review of grant programs, both designated and non-designated, will decide their assignment within the budget building process.

The lead time to enable a school district to adequately plan for and change over to school site budgeting would be between six months and a year, depending on the available opportunities for in-service training of staff, the competencies of the district support staff, data processing capabilities, the public information dissemination process, and the necessary political ambience.

School Business Official

Since this is a system for improved financial planning, the district business office needs to be understanding and supportive of the splintered, de- centralized nature of the sources of future budget building information.

The first task will be to compare the proposed school site budgets with the format of the existing

151

budgets and to conceptualize the necessary submission forms for the schools. Separate groupings of data are required for (1) personnel and (2) materials. A third grouping may be set up in order to monitor support service activities if desirable. The school site budget forms may assume the same expenditure categories as the present budgetary system (by program, function, object, or activity) and need not adjust to any other transformation. But, where options exist, it would be advisable to design the forms in a logical sequence to best assist the school building budgetary effort. By requesting only minimal input information, the forms need not become a cumbersome imposition on school clerical capabilities. The central business office need not require extensive categorical sub-totals such as can later be attained from a data processing center. The schools will be further aided if unit costs are contained on the forms and only the desired quantities need be added by school budget preparers, i.e. ____ secretaries @ $10,420 each.

The first simulation required is to re-cast the present budget in a school site budgeting format in order to develop ratios and rules for assignment of future school allotments.

Early in the planning stages there needs to be a determination of what items will be accommodated in the basic budget section and what items will be deferred to school site budgets. While it is desirous to assign as many items as possible to the domain of school buildings, there are some items that are not controllable or assignable to single school buildings in any logical fashion. Those items constitute the basic budget section.

After identifying the items that will be centrally (basic) budgeted, a financial summary of them as contained in the present budget should be assembled. After subtracting the basic budget costs from the total current appropriation for school purposes, the remainder provides the money available for assignment to schools for their building planning activities.

The next task is to determine what pupil weighting allocations will be established. For children requiring exceptional programs, a model can be constructed by assigning resources as required for each pathology.

Then, by determining the added costs due to smaller staff ratios and extensive support services, a relationship to the cost of schooling average students may be established.

The ratios for grade level assignments are determined by examining several years of fund assignments to schools of varying grade levels. If kindergarten programs are operated for only a half day, the pupil count for kindergarten pupils would be .5. If secondary schools have been spending 25% more than elementary schools (per capita) for the past several years, each secondary school pupil would get an assigned value of 1.25. To refine the estimate of resources previously assigned to secondary schools, it would first be necessary to compute the average teacher salary for the entire school district and apply it to the number of elementary and secondary school positions. By totalling the averaged salary value and dividing it by the number of pupils serviced, a refined estimate of the secondary school pupil weighting differential may be obtained.

If there are schools of disparate size, it may be desirable to apply a size subsidy to enable the smaller schools to continue to provide adequate supervisory, clerical, and custodial services without overly burdening their small per capita base allowance. This is done by determining such expenditures within the median enrollment school and assigning an equivalent funding subsidy for each pupil below the district building median.

By developing a summary chart of all pupils, including weightings for special programs and grade level differentials, a total number of weighted pupil expenditure units (WPEU) is amassed. The WPEU are divided into the total amount available for school site budgeting (less the size subsidy set-aside), and a simulated per capita expenditure amount is derived. The per capita sum is then assigned to each building, based on anticipated enrollment of each category of pupils.

Average current salaries are calculated for each classification of school employee and published in a list format.

Each school building leader is now to be engaged in a simulation exercise of applying assigned funding and pupil assignment data along with this year's average salaries to construct a model of how the funds might have been allocated within each building. This exercise, while being redundant to the existing spending plan, will point out the advantages and potential problems of school site budgeting planning assumptions, proposed documentation, and overall understanding of the process.

School Building Leaders

The first response to receiving a lot of new found autonomy is likely to be of a favorable nature, followed quickly by reminisences of the Trojan horse epic. Since the initial experience will be one of simulating the present budget in a school site decision format, the administrators' curiosity provides the motivation for constructively examining the benefits and problems that will unfold. Without the development of inexpensive pocket calculators the school site budgetary process may not have become a viable alternative. Such calculators become an everyday tool of school building administrators who wish to control their school expenditure allocations.

Student grouping is the first consideration. By placing the students into specific classes and assigning staff members to each such class, a summary of needed staff positions is achieved. The biggest single issue of budgetary planning at the school building level is the number of professional staff members to be employed. Approximately 95% of available funding will be required for professional staffing. After the other staffing has been determined, less than 3% of building level allocations will remain for supplies, materials and other services.

Building administrators must employ considerable leadership skill in involving school community members in planning for their future. The touchstone continues to be that of pupil welfare, though staff members may continue to press for matters of job security, and working conditions. Building leaders, by sharing information to show the equality of fund assignment on a district-wide basis, openly invite staff participation in achieving the maximum gain from the assigned resources. Ideally, creative planning will produce

154

exceptional local decisions that will provide unique and customized arrangements. The addition or deletion of a single professional position may involve $20,000-$25,000 to be available for other purposes. Or the shifting of non-teaching duties to para-professionals may realize some funding gains. Since the funds are exclusively earmarked for each school, any displaced funds may be used for any locally determined school purpose. Only two funding use ground rules are required, (1) funds must be used to meet district objectives, and (2) standard average salary rates or contracted hourly rates must be used when planning position allocations. Schools are not permitted to promulgate pay scales. Local restrictions may exist for class sizes or working conditions as specified in labor agreements. But generally, schools are permitted and encouraged to develop their unique budgetary planning solutions. Monies remaining after all staff decisions are made would be assignable to supplies, materials, and other resources.

Being a simulation exercise, certain conclusions of planning adequacies may be drawn. Most likely, using a similar amount of funding to provide the current program would cause no great deviation from that which exists. However, given a clean slate for future planning purposes, school building leaders become enthused over the possibilities of creating an improved educational enterprise through the creative and customized application of assignable funds.

While being removed from the heretofore restrictions of a central planning authority, it soon becomes apparent that locally developed options need to be justifiable and substantiated. Some hard choices are required when class groupings hover around maximum or minimum sizes. Whether to add to or re-assign professional staffing in such borderline cases requires considerable skills of rationalization and profound leadership skills in order to convince others of the wisdom of the decision.

Final Shake-Down

When all of the school building simulation budgets have been completed and reviewed, some fine tuning adjustments may be required. If assigned funds are excessive or deficient for any school or program,

155

modifications may be made to the assumptions which produced the apparent discrepancy. Adjustments generally take one or two forms. Either the items relegated to the basic section of the budget are increased or decreased or the weightings assigned to pupil characteristics are altered. To add or subtract items to the basic budget section will change the amount of funding available for local building budgetary planning. When categories of expenditures are assigned to the basic budget section their funding and accomplishment is somewhat assured. When such expenditures are relegated to school unit planning, their achievement becomes subject to local interpretation and priorities. Schools may accomplish the desired outcomes in a more efficient manner or may discover a way of combining or altering the function for costs savings. Or, it may prove more costly to splinter some district-wide obligations into school funding planning modes.

A greater impact on school building fund adequacies will result from the pupil weighting assumptions. The mix of elementary and secondary school expenditures is the trickiest element of starting a school site budgeting process. The only way of establishing such a relationship is to review their funding proximity for each of several preceding years and to have a dry run simulation of the tentative weighting assignments. The district policy makers and central administrative authority may deliberately opt to alter the relationship that has prevailed. Through control of funding allocations, school offerings can be directly governed.

Upon final adjustment of the planning components, a go or no-go decision is established. The reader is reminded that school site budgeting is a process for simulating a school budget through the use of average salaries. It enables planning to take place in an idealistic fashion, wholly dependent upon student needs. It does not supplant the legally required school district budget that is to be produced in conventional format. Rather, it is a process for obtaining improved customized allocation of the district's resources. Policy decisions are yet made at the highest level, district goals and objectives are yet established at the level of the chief administrative officer, and instructional decisions are now made at the instructional (school) level.

156

Chapter 13

PUTTING IT ALL TOGETHER

School building budgets are compiled in a dual fashion. All materials and services are listed at their best known costs, and all salaries are listed at the simulated group average for each classification of employee. The central business office has the task of replacing average salaries with actual salaries for each employee. When both tangible goods and services and employee salaries are expressed in real costs, the next step is one of assembling those items in a conventional budget review format. Usually, a legislated or historic format is prescribed. By using a consistent format, budget reviewers have a familiarity with the displays and have the advantage of like data for multi-year comparative purposes.

A line item budget proposal would show each proposed expenditure in isolation, thus providing maximum exposure for the validation of each recommendation. While such an arrangement provides the clearest display of detailed information, it has the disadvantage of promulgating an unfathomable quantity of isolated entities. Contemporary data processing capabilities can generate an infinite array of trivial data which tend to confound meaningful absorption of instructional program efforts. Such information is more commonly grouped by function or program in order to assist the reviewer. By definition, function or program expressions are virtually interchangeable, although either term may be defined to connote a broader or narrower conception. Assuming that individual schools have assembled their data in terms of instructional programs, it is necessary to re-assemble their allocations into consolidated district-wide programs, and to list aggregate expenditures by objects or items within the programs.

At the point in time when the schools have submitted their finalized budget documents, the central business office should be able to add the schools' budgets to the basic costs budget and produce the total budget package as previously agreed. An orderly conversion process is required to assure that all school decisions are accurately transformed into the budget proposal of the school district.

157

When the separate school budgets are submitted to the central business office, they must be screened for completeness and their data need to be verified. Since the overall budget target was previously affixed, individual schools must neither exceed nor fall short of their allotments. Schools normally use a discretionary supply or materials account to force a zero balance. Nevertheless, the school business office needs to ascertain that proper salary rates are incorporated and that all mathematical extensions and accumulations are precise. Such computations are eased if prescribed salary rates are pre-printed on the school budget preparation forms.

Transformation of School Budgetary Plans

When all school budget data are verified, the personnel entries may be culled out and re-assembled in district program format. For the first time, the central office administrators will learn of the final number of employees that have been provided in each category of the work force. Since all schools have projected positions at the prevailing average salaries, the net total of positions, though changed by school options, will be affordable. If a net decline in the number of positions is indicated, the business office will remove the salaries of the least senior persons in each program. The reader is reminded that this budget planning process occurs many months in advance of the period it provides for. If, as a result of the school expenditure elections, several teaching positions are unnecessary within a given instructional program, the central business office constructs a budget model without those several positions. In the intervening months between budget planning and budgetary implementation, there may be sufficient staff attrition to offset the school-opted reductions. The least senior staff members of a program may not be the lowest paid persons within the program. Recently hired persons with advanced degrees may have rates of pay above more senior staff members having less preparation. On the other hand, if the aggregate number of positions within a program are to be increased as a result of school funding assignments, the central business office may plan to add the indicated number of positions at the district average salary. This assumes that a balanced range of experience is desired among new personnel. The school district might also assume a defensible

posture that newly hired staff members will be sought
from persons of limited experience who may be more
readily molded by the district's in-service training
program. That being the case, new positions may be
entered in the district budget at a below average salary,
closer to that of the beginning end of prevailing wage
scales.

Due to the timing of such late adjustments caused
by increasing or decreasing staff members, the finalized
district budget will achieve a slightly different total
than the school budgets. The schools' budgets were
constructed with simulated (average) salaries and the
district budget will be cast in actual salaries, modified by refined rates for added or deleted positions.
Other phenomenon which will change the total funding
package between school and district budgets are variations required to round off work assignments split
between several separate school buildings and by either
the duplication of fringe benefits for two half time.
assignments or the absence of fringe benefits for
fractional assignments not totalling to a whole position. The average of differences that occur during
the transformation of school budgets may be absorbed
or credited to any of the discretionary supply,
materials, or reserve accounts within the basic budget
planning section.

Upon completion of the conversion process all
authorized (budgeted) positions are assigned to district
programs at their actual salaries and only known vacancies are carried at an assumed salary rate. Positions
that were contained within the basic costs budget section are also carried over and combined with school
budgeted positions and unified to form the district
budget programs.

As an internal control test device, it is
recommended that all wage amounts be summarized and
compared to the initial group totals that were used
to establish the average salary rates used for the
construction of school budgets. Due to some split
assignments (less travel time) the total salary blocks
may differ slightly. Such tests provide the timely
opportunity to verify the consistency of the salary
handling procedures. Errors of transformation,
transposition, or juxtaposition can more easily be
identified, isolated, reconciled, and remedied at
this juncture.

Transforming Supplies and Materials Accounts

The amounts set aside by each school for the purchase of supplies, materials, and services must be transformed to the district budget and listed within applicable programs. Normally, there are no adjustments to these data and they are entered intact. Similar items provided within the basic costs budget section are likewise entered in the overall district program format. Items coming from (1) schools, or (2) basic budget may be combined in the district budget or for purposes of monitoring may continue to be separately listed. The advantage of combining the elements is that of fewer separate accounts. School site budgeting generally causes a large increase in the number of accounts to be maintained. Since there is some cost associated with creating and monitoring separate accounts, the practitioner must determine whether the advantages of cost monitoring are proportionate to the additional account maintenance costs.

Check and Balance

When all salary, supportive service, and materials costs have been assigned to district programs, a trial balance should be taken in order to test the thoroughness and accuracy of the conversion process. The task will be lightened if a separate test was made after all salary transformations were achieved. If the district budget in its legislated format agrees with the total of the basic costs and school assigned costs, the school site budgetary process is complete and all the simulation activities are ended. From that point on the school district will deal exclusively in actual wages, costs, benefits, and expenditures.

Producing a Meaningful Budget Document

When preparing a finalized budget document, the originator needs to consider the nature of the persons who will be reading, assessing, and taking some action or mind set as a result of receiving the document. While the budget document must be technically correct, it must also communicate the rationale to support the proposed expenditure elements.

To achieve maximum impact, the budgetary data should be assembled in at least two dimensions. First, the school site budgets (and basic costs section) should be presented in full, enabling the reader to see how each school responded to the planning task. If each school's data can be condensed onto a single page, the reader may quickly achieve an executive overview. Meaningful conclusions can be drawn if at least two columns of data are provided, one for the current year, and one for the (upcoming) year covered by this planning cycle. Trends or changes in emphases can be quickly spotted and comprehended. The single page should contain all essential data of the four elements of a school site budget (1) enrollment, (2) staffing, (3) materials and services, and (4) other costs. A few well conceived comparative ratios may be generated for each school site budget. Such relationships as average class size/grade, pupil/staff, teaching/support staff, administrative/teaching, staff costs/ per capita, materials costs/per capita, support staff costs/per capita, all tend to make the data more lucid for purposes of inter-school comparisons. The practitioner may further isolate data for comparative purposes on the basis of academic subjects or school program arrays. Second only to its mission as a fiscal planning device, the budget serves as a communications medium. As such it should reveal rather than conceal information about the schools!

Along with the numerical expression of a school's plans, some explanation of the rationale for such funding assignments would be beneficial. Each school unit should provide a one page summary describing priorities as established by building administrators and staff, and by parents and other interested members of the community. In some cases, student input may also contribute to the planning of program priorities. Such purposes may be expressed as goals, objectives, or priorities, but at the outset of the planning process some uniformity of style should be encouraged in order to facilitate the comprehension of the consumer. In addition to numeric facts and program priorities, an element of growth or improvement would be a desirable entity in each school's budget summary. Such a section (paragraph) should describe plans for program improvement, growth, expansion, enrichment, change, or new opportunities that will become available. If the priorities and goals of each school are expressed in a narrative fashion void of statistical or numeric descriptors, a more understandable presentation is likely to occur.

If the school site/basic cost budget does not ful-
fill the mandated requirements of a budget format
required for funding consideration, a second complete
budget, in proper format, may be provided between the
same covers. The second (conventional) budget may also
be enhanced by flagging district-wide program features
that have been promulgated by the central school district administrative influence. The decentralized
autonomous budget building process of each school is
yet orchestrated and guided by the common goals and
instructional objectives that are centrally prescribed.
Their publication within the conventional budget format
would round out the reviewer's knowledge of (1) building
level planning efforts, and (2) district level planning
efforts.

The budget document should be made more readable
by the omission of a series of digits that ordinarily
preface an account. Such numbers are only meaningful
to an account analyzer or a data processing facility.
While such account codes may be eliminated from the
budget prepared for public consumption, they are
necessarily maintained for record handling purposes,
generally in the form of a Work Budget, housed at the
school business office. Copies of the finalized
Work Budget are provided to each school after all
details are resolved and funded. The schools rely
on the Work Budget to set up their internal accounts
and to properly assign expenditure transactions. Their
periodic account reports will also be transmitted in the
format consistent with the Work Budget.

Because of the large numbers associated with school
budgets, it is difficult to make meaningful comparisons
with like expenditures in government, industry, domestic
or religious or fraternal organizational budgets.
In order to explain the reasons for budget funding
levels, the compiler must provide useful comparative
data. The following list illustrates many readily
available statistics that can be gathered and presented
in understandably graphic fashion.

        enrollment
        wealth, assessments, tax rate
        source of revenues
        percentages of increases
        salary schedules
        cost trends - supplies, materials, utilities

yardstick comparisons with other districts
state comparisons, expenditures, wealth, staffing
grants
test scores
scholarship awards
follow-up studies of graduates
rental of school building facilities
class size
drop outs, retentions, attendance
pupils transported, field trips, cost/mile,
cost/passenger
library circulation
personnel - preparation and certification
in-service programs
energy consumption trends
long range plan - short range plan
inventory - fixed, variable
property values
staff preparation
debt service
investment performance

To maximize the gain from a well developed budget,
a concise table of contents should appear at the beginning of the document. Account summaries, conveniently
placed on the inside front cover or outside back cover
(or both) will enable the user to get a quick overview
of the budget proposal and to identify items of particular interest for further review. In the type of
budget/s suggested herein, the reader can examine plans
as detailed as each class within each school building
or as gross as a district's broad aggregate efforts.

In the commercial sector, the goal of budgetary
planning is to improve the company's profit making
capacity. In the public sector, the goal of budgetary
planning is to maximize the effectiveness of programs
that are being provided. Abstract planning is of
limited value until it is augmented by financial considerations. Schools, using money as a motivational
vehicle, produce improved expenditure planning by
first parcelling resources for individual school
buildings and encouraging their creative resolution
of homebred problems.

Chapter 14

MAKING THE MOST OF DATA PROCESSING

Contrary to popular notion, computers may not impersonalize the fulfillment of human needs and wants. Quite the opposite is more likely to occur as computers handle countless bits of information in order to individualize responses to specific situations. With manual processing of information, the number of exceptions was limited to the size of the files to be maintained or the memory or manipulative capabilities of the human processor. The limits of machine processing are as boundless as the nature of their control programs and a storage capacity which approaches infinity. Such terms as drone, slave, or robot are often employed to describe the computers' unbounded capacity to handle repetitive data and select and indicate predetermined conclusions with total accuracy. These characteristics of a data processing function are precisely the reasons that data processing will permit, foster, and accommodate school site budgeting.

While school accounting lends itself to systemization, there has been limited effort to develop functional state-wide data processing routines that would be compatable with the processing capabilities of school districts. In the absence of such a universal system, local school districts have independently produced workable processing routines. Sometimes such multiple efforts have produced redundancy and inefficiency while ignoring economies of scale.

Ideally, state-wide management information systems would provide standardized forms and procedures that would (1) provide uniformity of data, (2) obtain needed information, (3) provide for local activity monitoring options, (4) permit machine reporting in coded data format, (5) allow the local school districts of the network to trade comparable data, (6) create timely and accurate feed-back, (7) be an accurate facilitator of grants and special funds, (8) encourage uniform auditing procedures, (9) develop appropriate forms and formats, and (10) provide an infinite variety of data for future applications.

For the few states that have made progress towards the development of a unified data processing system, it is likely that accounting activities may be traced to a single school, even if not presently required. Systems planners typically envision future requirements and would not overlook the eventual monitoring of small scale activities. In order to assure that resources are reaching each student, state-wide educational accounting systems must be expanded to reflect building (and sometimes class or grade level) fiscal activities.

School site budgeting would be very difficult to install and maintain without the aid of a machine assisted data processing capability. Data processing services are often furnished to schools by local governmental agencies. Small school districts have several choices for acquiring data processing services. They may purchase services from a service bureau or a time-sharing service facility, or may obtain affordable services from nearby banking, commercial, industrial, or (possible regional) educational data centers. Another option would be that of purchasing a micro computer for the price of about two typewriters, or the purchase a mini computer for only slightly more.

Microcomputers

When schools acquire microcomputers, several user friendly programs are available to aid the building level budgetary process. The handiest type of accounting program is the spread sheet format, enabling novice users to design extensive interconnected rows and columns of numeric data. When any elements of the array are altered, all of the other components are instantly re-calculated to incorporate the change and provide updated cumulative data. One step up from spread sheets would be a range of data base management programs available for microcomputers. These require more planning and mastery of the concepts of system processing. The user can set up screen formats, files, and data banks, and can assemble, sort, compare, merge, or list an infinite variety of information. The other popular type of programs for microcomputers are the word processing programs that enable rapid and flexible handling of text. Some word processing programs also have the capability of four function mathematical computation and optional accessories such as a thesaurus which provides lists of synonyms, or a dictionary that scans the text for spelling or hyphenation errors and highlights any words that vary from the stored conformation. Word processing programs are especially useful when they are compatible (will interface) with data base or file handling systems, allowing the user to merge other data with the text. While the initial set up of microcomputer routines may be time consuming, future recall for the preparation of subsequent budgets is instantaneous.

Account Codes

A small boy, having but two pockets in his trousers, can easily account for his possessions, left or right side. A multi-million dollar school system has an infinite number of pockets where resources may be placed. To maximize their use, or to even locate them, a system of pocket identification (accounting) is required. The system must be comprehensive, complete, logically derived, and consistently applied. Otherwise, items will be lost, untraceable, mislaid, misappropriated, or in an otherwise chaotic state.

The U.S. Department of Education has attempted to provide a school accounting system that would be useful throughout the nation. The recently revised Handbook II, Financial Accounting for Local and State School Systems, provides a standard terminology, but the system has not yet been adopted by all the States. For purposes of illustration, this discussion of establishing an accounting system for each school building will adhere to the general provision of that system. The handbook was published in 1957 and revised in 1973 and 1980.

The handbook classifies assets and other debits, revenues, and expenditures. It is this latter phase of classification (expenditures) which will be most useful in launching a school site budgeting process.

In developing or adopting a standardized accounting classification system, the first concern is the purpose or reason for which something exists or is to be used. The function and program designation incorporates four digits, or 9999 program possibilities. It is unlikely that a school district would exceed 999 functions or programs. The prefixed digit indicates a broad category of function: Instruction, Support Services, Operation of Non-Instructional Services, Facilities Acquisition and Construction Services, and Other Uses.

Consider the function of Regular Instruction with an account code of 1000. This provides 999 possibilities or places that may be used to designate programs of instruction (1001-1999). By using an abbreviated version from another governmental manual, Standard Terminology for Curriculum and Instruction in Local and State School Systems, one can produce a series of account codes to designate each curriculum and program area. For example:

1000 Regular Instruction
1001 Agriculture
1002 Art
1003 Business Education
1004 Distributive Education
1005 English Language Arts
1006 Foreign Language
1007 Health Occupations
1008 Health & Safety, Physical Education, Recreation
1009 Home Economics
1010 Industrial Arts
1011 Mathematics
1012 Music
1013 Natural Sciences
1014 Office Occupations
1015 Social Sciences, Social Studies
1016 Technical Education
1017 Trade and Industrial Occupations

The 1200 series of accounts is designated for Special Education Programs (gifted, handicapped, exceptional) and the 1300 series of accounts is designated for Vocational Education programs. Adult/Continuing Education programs are assigned to a 1600 series of accounts, and Community Services are listed at 1800. The 2000 series provides a range of program identifiers for Support Services:

2100 Pupil Services
2110 Attendance and Social Work Services
2120 Guidance Services
2130 Health Services
2140 Psychological Services
2150 Speech Pathology & Audiology Services

168

2200	Support Services - Instructional Staff
2210	Improvement of Instruction Services
2220	Educational Media Services
2310	Board of Education Services
2320	Executive Administration Services
2400	Support Services - School Administration
2500	Support Services - Business
2600	Operation and Maintenance of Plant Services
2700	Pupil Transportation Services
2800	Support Services - Central
2840	Data Processing Services
3100	Food Service Operations

Normally, the 1000 and 2000 series of activities accounts will provide for most functions or programs utilized in the planning of a school building budget. The intervening account numbers are available for local assignment to monitor other functions.

To re-cap, a series of four digits is utilized to designate the function or program for which expenditures are to be made. Whenever information is needed about the schools' Art program, for example, the data processing system will be asked to search through and cull out all accounts that have a designation of 1002. In response to such an inquiry, all expenditures for Art will be isolated and ready for review or for subsequent commands.

The next order of command will be to identify objects or things that are to be purchased for the Art program. This requires three additional digits and within the Handbook the series are shown as:

100	Salaries
200	Benefits
300	Purchased Professional and Technical Services

```
                    400 Purchased Property
                        Services
                    500 Other Purchased Services
                    600 Supplies
                    700 Property
                    800 Other Objects
```

The blank (00) second and third digits of the above series are locally assignable to specific objects of expenditures. For example:

```
100  Salaries                101 Superintendent of Schools
                             102 Assistant Superintendents
                             103 Directors
                             104 Supervisors
                             105 Coordinators
                             110 Principals
                             112 Assistant Principals
                             114 Counselors
                             116 Social Workers
                             126 Career Specialist
                             133 Librarian
                             135 Media Specialist
                             140 Teachers
                             150 Secretaries
                             155 Aides
                             160 Foods Service Workers
                             165 Custodians
                             170 Maintenance Workers
                             175 Bus Drivers
```

The open numbers between such categories remain available for future growth or expansion of position designations.

The 300 series of objects shows:

```
                    300 Technical & Professional
                        Services
                    310 Official/Administrative
                        Services
                    320 Professional-Educational
                        Services
                    330 Other Professional
                        Services
                    340 Technical Services
```

The 400 series of objects defines Purchased Property Services:

410 Utility Services
420 Cleaning Services
430 Repairs & Maintenance Services
440 Rentals
450 Construction Services

Other Purchased Services are provided for within the 500-700 series of object designations:

510 Student Transportation Services
520 Insurance
530 Communications
540 Advertising
550 Printing & Binding
560 Tuition
570 Food Service Management
580 Travel
600 Supplies
620 Energy
630 Food
640 Books and Periodicals
700 Property
730 Equipment

So far, the accounting system has provided a designation for an Art Program and Supplies within that program:

```
    ┌····· 1002 - 600 ·····┐
    :                      :
  Art Program         Supplies
```

Asking the computer to list all expenditures for Art supplies throughout the district would require a seeking, sorting, and reporting in the above command sequence.

A third grouping of digits will bring the account classification system to a single building location (cost center) or a level of a generalized service. The third series within an account code may contain 2 or 3 digits depending upon the number of separate school buildings, cost centers, operational units, or service levels desired. One such array would show:

171

```
02   Pre-School
03   Elementary Level
04   Middle/Jr. High Level
05   Senior High Level
06   Secondary Schools
07   All Schools
08   Grades K - 8
09   Unassigned
```
```
10 to 60   Elementary Schools
61 to 70   Junior High/Middle Schools
71 to 80   High Schools
81 to 99   Other Buildings
```

Completing the example of account groupings:

```
..........1002 - 600 - 17.........
```

Art Program   Supplies   Wilson Elementary School

The computer has thus culled out all activity in the account related to Art Supplies in the Wilson Elementary School. With equal facility, the computer could be made to produce data in any combination of Function, Object, or Location. So long as each transaction is keyed to such an accounting codification system, it will always be recallable by the digit-seeking computer program. The only addition to the standardized function-object accounting system is that of building or building level codes assignment. Once they are devised, a full blown school site budgeting process can be machine produced.

It is also possible to further expand the accounting system to show grade level or even classroom expenditures. Generally, the burden of maintaining data on such a wide scale negates its desirability. It is relatively simple to carry account designations to the building level. Then, if a process or activity needs monitoring within the building, only the isolated building data need to be scrutinized. For the few occasions when such detail is desired, it seems easier to research it after the fact rather than everlastingly maintain it in a state of unneeded readiness.

Personnel Data

When beginning to tool up for a school site approach to budgeting, it is necesary to calculate the average (mean) salary for each classification of

employees. By using average salaries to construct
school site budgets, the budgets are not randomly
skewed by the degree and longevity based salary
schedules. There is the added advantage of preserving
staff morale by not isolating staff members for examination on the sole criteria of earnings. The budgets
are to be planned on the basis of number of positions,
predicated on average salaries for each type of position.
See Table 4.3. Note: this simulation of salaries is
only used for budget planning and assembly of school
unit costs. The finalized budget for funding consideration will be re-assembled and presented with actual
salaries of individuals. And throughout the fiscal
year, all accounting will occur in actual dollar
allocations and expenditures.

The typical personnel categories for establishing
average annual salaries for planning purposes may
include:

> Principals
> Assistant Principals
> Directors
> Supervisors
> Coordinators
> Teachers
> Nurses
> Aides
> Secretaries
> Custodians

and any other categories of school employees. Separate
averages need to be established for each group that
functions under a different pay scale. Also, the length
of the employment periods (10 months, 11 months, 12
months) require differing salary averages. When properly coded, the data processing system will generate
such affinity groups and calculate the average wage
and benefit costs for each group. To do this, the
computer must first sort by the object code that
identifies a class of positions. The computer may
then be directed to assemble current salaries or may
have next year's salary schedules entered and applied
to each constituent. In so doing, the computer can
simultaneously advance the salaries of those employees
scheduled to receive a wage increment. Then, by
dividing the accumulated total by the number of entries,
an average salary is provided for the upcoming budget

building process. The computer will also assemble the average cost of employee benefits for each person of the grouping. Just as with salaries, benefit costs are averaged for budget building simulations and ultimately re-cast into actual costs in the finalized (to be funded) budget document.

Enrollment

The continuous accounting for pupils is a ready task for a data processing system. The number of students and their various characteristics, including special instructional requirements, will serve as the basis of per capita appropriations to school buildings. Since school population census requirements have been rigidly imposed since the enactment of child labor laws, and since many states dispense financial aid on the basis of such data, the codification and processing procedures for gathering and monitoring such information are in place.

School site budgeting requires the equivalent assignment of funds to schools on the basis of number of pupils to be served. Also, the process provides differentiated funds for pupils who have exceptional needs. The weightings that are provided for exceptional pupils are further refinements made possible by a comprehensive data processing system. However, if the number of such exceptions is small, it may not be feasible to program a computer just for that purpose. Most likely, however, their exceptionality is available in a data bank already required by state and federal mandates regarding the programmatic accounting for handicapped students.

Long range enrollment forecasts are generally predicated by a data processing unit that gathers and analyzes a chronology of student population as a basis for future expectations. Such data are valuable when using school site budgeting to simulate conditions up to five years in advance. By synthesizing the future, preparations can be made to cope with expected enrollment and/or expenditure requirements. The data base system can accurately and effortlessly maintain all the mundane requisite information and calculations. Five years is a realistically predictive interval since all students who will enter kindergarten in five years have already been born. Beyond five years, predictability requires analyses of probable birth rates, sociological and economic conditions, migratory phenomena, and retention/promotion policies.

Accumulation of School Data

The schools, being provided with estimates of future enrollment and with funding levels based on the projected enrollment, set about the task of determining how the money may be best utilized. A series of decisions are arrived at and dollar values are assigned to personnel (at simulated average salaries) and other services, materials, and supplies (at actual costs). Such school data may be assembled by grade level or program format. Elementary schools may develop budgets primarily in grade level format and secondary schools in program format. This arrangement acknowledges the typical self contained classroom concept of elementary schools. Secondary schools are more apt to assemble costs by program in the first instance and by grade level only for selected statistical purposes. This arrangement acknowledges the typical specialized subject centered instructional arrangement prevalent in secondary schools.

School budget preparation forms are designed to be compatible with the aforementioned accounting code system. The data processing center can absorb each school's expenditure options classified by programs and objects. In so doing, total allocations are instantly verified for conformance with the overall appropriation. A check for concordance can be made to verify the school's exclusive and accurate utilization of posted simulated average salaries. Statistical summaries of personnel and materials ratios may be extracted and compared with similar information from other schools. Examination of such ratios and proportions permit executive confirmation of the balanced nature of school allocations. Also, since the budget preparation form shows expenditures for the present year in addition to the proposed future year, the computer can compare and contrast and illuminate all significant variations between successive years.

Next, the computer is directed to assemble the school budgets into a summary review format by program, by object, by location, by grade level, or by any combination of these dimensions. Budget reviewers are aided in their understanding of component relationships within and between separate school budget plans by having instant access to rank summary or juxtaposed data. Conclusions may also be achieved by examining

175

prior year data to establish an understanding of linear
trends in staffing, student program elections, materials
and supply acquisitions, and schedule modifications.

At some point, the school budgets are merged with
the basic costs budget section in order to display and
verify the complete school site budgeting package.
When it appears that the allocations are finalized, the
data center is directed to convert the school site
budget/s to the conventional format for final legislative
funding review.

First, all the personnel changes require validation.
The data processing unit has the bench mark salary data
from which the average salaries were derived. The
schools used those average salaries in assigning personnel within the limits of their separate appropriations. Upon summarizing the various classifications of
employees listed in each school's budget, the total
number of positions in each job category is known. If
it turns out that the schools have elected to employ the
same number of positions as currently existing in any
category, the data center need not alter that roster.
If, however, the schools opt to employ fewer positions
in any job category, the data base must be made to
reflect the changes. Guided by extant labor agreement
reduction in force provisions, the least senior staff
members (actual salaries) are removed from the data
base in sufficient number to match the declining jobs
assigned within school budgets. If conversely the
schools have elected to employ additional persons in
any job category, provisions must be made by adding
vacant positions to those job rosters. Such vacancies
are to be funded at either best known expected hiring
salaries or at the previously simulated average salary
for the particular job category.

Note the difference in budgeted salary assumptions
depending on whether positions are being deleted or
expanded. When deleting positions, the district average
salary may not be used, since most labor agreements
contain a reduction in force provision with some element
of seniority attached. Thus, persons of average salary
and likely having 15 years of experience, will not
normally be let go. The last persons hired are the
most likely targets for position elimination. A way
of treating the phenomena of staff decline as triggered
by pupil population decline is to estimate the loss of

positions at the time the average salaries are first calculated. If, for example, it appears that a pupil population decline of 200 students will result in a net reduction of ten teaching positions, the least costly ten teaching positions may be lopped off the roster before average salaries are calculated. Thus, each school will use a slightly inflated salary average but the eventual reduction of those positions (at actual salaries) will leave the data base intact and accurately reflecting the resulting diminution.

When providing additional positions as a result of school budgetary decisions, there is an option of planning for them at either actual or average salaries. If a school district seeks a balance of recent entry professionals and experienced professionals, the average salary will provide funds to achieve such selections. If a school district prefers to engage professionals at lower cost, the anticipated actual salary requirements (somewhat lower than district average salaries) may be entered into the data base.

Whether the number of positions diminish or increase in each job category, the data base for each group needs to be updated prior to conversion to the final funding format. When all such modifications have been made, the data are ready to be re-cast in almost any desired format. Since services, supplies, and materials costs were assigned to the schools in actual (not simulated) amounts, they require no modification or statistical treatment in preparation for re-formatting.

By ordering the computer to group and display all (both school site and basic budget) allocations in an assigned format, a comprehensive budget array will be produced. Persons who want to know more about school expenditures find such multiple displays to their satisfaction. The more common configuration of budgetary alignment would be by activity, program, function, line item or object and/or location (cost center). In some locales it is customary to group expenditures by (1) personnel and (2) other costs, or occasionally by (1) instructional, and (2) non-instructional costs. With appropriate assignment of expenditure account designations, a contemporary data processing facility could sort on any combination of the above factors plus age, grade, sex, neighborhood, race, ability, achievement,

177

mandated programs, contractual requirements, zero based operation .... The only requirement would be to anticipate a future need for such groupings and be certain that the accounting code is sufficiently broad to provide a tag designation for each such entity. The computer's major advantage over a large and well planned filing system is its capacity to assemble information, make an infinite number of trials of contrast and comparison, and to select or amplify the response indicated by pre-supposed phenomena or conditions. And, the computer never gets tired, bored, lazy, sloppy, slow, inaccurate, overworked, misunderstood, or deviates in any way from rigidly prescribed logical responses to given circumstances.

Accounting For Expenditures

After the budget planning activity is completed, the well designed data handling system becomes an important aid for expenditure accounting. The same data sorting and assembling capabilities enables the user to review expenditures grouped by cost centers (schools), by programs, by functions, by activities, by objects, or in terms of any particular segment that needs to be monitored. Accounting reports illustrate the current status of each account including the expenditures, encumbrances, and unencumbered balances. The account report should also indicate any adjustments (increases, decreases, or transfers) to or from each account. And upon request, the data center can provide a summary of all previous transactions in detail. Such accumulations serve as a valued audit trail to review prior performance.

Information regarding expenditures may be obtained in print format (financial statements) or by being displayed on a cathode ray tube (CRT) for visual access. The user may decide whether it is sufficient to merely view and possibly change data via a CRT or whether it is essential that hard (printed) copy is required. Concepts of paperless offices, however, project the demise of hard copy materials and the growth of visual access via video screens. Each cost center or office unit may have either a CRT terminal to a larger central computer, or may soon have separate micro processors interconnected through a common network centrally programmed with universal interface so that all can freely exchange information in the same format.

Expenditure accounting is required for report purposes and for analysis of operations. Specially funded grant programs require verification of expenditure activities, sometimes requiring the added dimension of comparability of like activities and/or maintenance of effort. There are often restrictions that grant monies may not be co-mingled with other funds or may not be used to displace or supplant other funding efforts. Without a complete data handling system, the administration of such grant restrictions would be extremely burdensome. A well conceived data processing system will provide an infinite variety of data which would be useful for planning activities.

Inherent in the design of data networks is a series of security controls. Users may be assigned passwords which will enable them to penetrate specific levels of accounting activity. Each user only has access to a given sphere of information. And each transaction is traceable to a specific operator via an internal audit trail. Such controls are required in order to prevent intrusion into sensitive data banks and to pin-point the source of errors, miscalculations, or fradulent data entry.

School site budgeting has only recently become a viable process for planning, governing, and managing the operation of an entire school system. It has mostly been made possible through the creation of lower cost electronic calculators and readily available data processing systems. Given such support capability, the myriad data requirements become less onerous and more like a helpful ally, providing information in a timely, accurate, and useful manner.

Chapter 15

A SUMMARY OF BENEFITS

When a school site budgeting process is developed
within a school district, a number of advantages occur.
Throughout this volume many of the gains have been cited.
This chapter will re-cap the benefits to the many persons
who are affected by the school site budget planning process.

The very act of altering budget building procedures
will cause a new examination of the process elements of
a school district. Present practices are scrutinized.
An examination of lines of communication takes place.
Attention is focused on the relationships of existing
administrative structure. New relationships are developed. An extensive in-service development program is
required of staff members. A re-assessment of priorities
and goals is triggered. A vitality is infused into an
otherwise onerous and stultified budget building process.
And, in all of this, a positive thrust takes place as a
different planning process takes shape. Even the most
casual observer will ponder, "How will this new thing
affect me?". The following paragraphs tend to provide
a response to such a question.

Boards of Education

Faced with the need to get a great amount of information in an understandable form, boards of education find the school site budgeting process to be a
worthy ally. Each school unit has compiled information
on a like basis, making inter-school comparisons an
easy task. In addition, a few helpful bottom line
ratios are included to show staff and materials assignments on a per capita basis. Significantly, enrollment
data are shown in direct relationship to cost data,
enabling reviewers to examine both sides of the equation
Further, staffing data are shown alongside of enrollment
data, for easy comparison and analysis. The information
is packaged in a pithy and compact manner, accommodating
the limited time availability of lay leaders.

Armed with a large amount of straightforward
information, boards of education can assume an executive,
policy making role. The probable impact of their policies can be readily transposed into fiscal and operational terms. A lesser tendency to infringe on the daily

school level decisions is likely to take place, recognizing that school decisions, made with considerable community support, aptly reflect the views of the constituents and should not be lightly displaced. Freed of those details, the board's policy making role emerges.

When funding choices are made at the building level, they are also to be rationalized and defended at that level. If the choices are of a controversial nature, the board of education acts as an appelate body with the options of ratifying or vetoing the school level decisions. Being fully informed, having a reasonable time for deliberation, and applying district wide perspective, the decisions of the governing board are based on greater insight and are more readily accomplished.

School efforts to achieve district objectives are highlighted for review. Measures of accountability and process evaluation are provided. The relationship of costs and benefits come into focus. The power to alter programs through their funding sources provides the leverage sought by a policy making board of school district governors. Plans of individual schools can be altered prior to their operational enactment. An all around greater understanding of roles and responsibilities is fostered.

School site budgeting would be particularly accommodating of vouchers or tuition credit allowances if such subsidies were enacted. Inasmuch as each pupil receives earmarked allocations it would be easy to trace such allowances and assure their applicability. Whereas, without school site budgeting, such subsidies may be co-mingled with general support funding and not reach the intended recipients.

The Superintendent of Schools

As an intermediary between the policy making governing board and the operational leaders of individual schools, the superintendent of schools is in a position to build an important communication bridge. Good planning procedures are expected of school building leaders. Their effectiveness is evaluated by the superintendent. The policies of the school board provide overall direction, but the achievement of district goals demand specific responses. The success of the schools in achieving those objectives is a phenomena clearly observable by the superintendent of schools.

The act of decentralizing decision making causes a sharing of administrative responsibilities, and broadens the perspective of administrators of school buildings.

The superintendent of schools can promote change by establishing some budgeting ground rules. If specific funding assignments are required, the ensuing programs have no choice but to conform to the expenditure regimens. Hence, programs may be expanded, compressed, or otherwise altered in accordance with the designs of the superintendent of schools.

The process of school site budgeting permits unlimited simulation possibilities. The schools can be provided with alternate assumptions of funding levels, enrollment changes, grade groupings, staffing ratios, materiel limitations, housing accommodations, or administrative or organizational changes. The probable consequences of such assumptions can be inexpensively and quickly assessed. The superintendent of schools can promote involvement of many community members by insisting that school leaders confer and consult with parents and interested citizens. The ensuing decisions have broad based community support and are not suspect as self serving goals of professional administrators and teachers.

Building Leaders

Faced with the many publics to be served, the building level administrator is most likely to skillfully use the school site budgeting process to develop a customized response to board policy requirements. Decisions that are locally contrived will best fit the building level requirements.

The budget planning process provides a stage where various notions can be unveiled and examined. And with discussion, alteration, compromise and barter, improved planning takes place. Priorities are exposed. Values are tested. Concessions are granted. In all, a dynamic and cohesive planning experience occurs in a controlled setting. The controls are prescribed by

(1) board policies, (2) district objectives, (3) administrative regulations, (4) extant labor agreements, (5) prevailing laws, and (6) funding constraints. As a catalyst, the building leader can seize the opportunity for molding a unified posture. And, shared decisions have a self fulfilling prophesy.

The exploration of alternatives becomes a vibrant force in developing improved operational plans. Creative thinking often produces enriched solutions to mundane problems. If new programs can only be afforded by the displacement of existing programs, the pruning process will probably cull the weakest (program) element of the school.

Budgetary awareness is likely to be a year round happening. Since schools are granted some options to transfer funds during the year, interest is sustained. The budget becomes an everyday tool rather than a cyclical extravaganza. At the building level it is referred to as "our" budget rather than "their" (the central administrative office) budget.

Teachers

School site budgeting enables teachers to make choices regarding their daily instructional activities. Not only are material and text choices made at a building level, the trade-offs of field trips, enrichment activities, or dimensions of time allocations can be evaluated and elected. Teachers' point of view receives full consideration as they participate in planning their own destiny. Their needs are exposed and fully aired. Curricular options are made available with a view towards best meeting the needs of an exact group of students. While average solutions meet the full needs of average students, classroom teachers are in a position to provide precise responses to the divergent needs of all students.

Teachers receive prompt feedback from their budget planning activities. School budget building decisions are simultaneously communicated.

By openly assigning all potential funds to schools, each staff member is aware of the expenditure limits, without obfuscation of key elements.

Teachers are encouraged to practice their profession of diagnosing, prescribing, promoting, and evaluating the instructional effort. Circumscribed methodology and materials restrictions are abandoned to each teacher's judgement. The research of trial and response becomes an every day occurrence.

Students

The instigation of school site budgeting is likely to have little immediate impact on the daily regimen of students. The concept of individual attention has long been the lodestone of curriculum and program offerings. And, it is unlikely that immediate and wholesale abandonment of current materials is to take place as a result of the autonomous permissiveness of school site budgeting. However, a renewed sense of individual analysis should occur. Each student should receive equivalent resources and equivalent educational opportunities consistent with individual needs. Groupings should be invoked only for effectiveness of purpose rather than for economies of scale. In viewing individual pupil needs such local factors as class mix, historical patterns of grouping, time on task variables, learning style and modality, and peer relationships may be acknowledged and rejoined.

At the level of secondary schools, student electives, extra curricular activities, and enrichment opportunities are most apt to be affected by the introduction of the school site budgeting process. Again, the expenditure decisions are to be provoked by the best interests of individual students, as democratically conceived.

Parents

Working within the previously determined gross allocation for education, an opportunity is provided for parents, staff, and other school community personages to genuinely share in making expenditure decisions. Formerly, citizen participation was mostly present after the school budget had been formulated and was being presented in public to a legislative funding authority, too late for substantive changes. Potential school supporters were at best unsure or uninformed of the budget contents, or how or why items were included or excluded during the formulation process.

185

In contrast, school site budgeting provides meaningful up-front involvement in developing program and expenditure decisions. Having wrestled with a series of elements competing for available resources, citizens are prepared to discuss and defend the results of their planning. Thus, legislative units will obtain a perspective rendered by convinced lay persons as well as administrative professionals. And, those citizens will be able to closely identify with and rationally support the expenditure proposals, having been involved and immersed in the formulation process.

A by-product of citizen participation in such a fish bowl atmosphere is the public confidence that all budgeted allocations are singularly essential. By exposing all available resources and completing a process of critical selection, there can be no spectre of waste, redundance, or inflation (padding) of budgetary items.

In this regimen the legislative hearing of an appropriation for school purposes need not focus on a budget that needs to be defended, reduced, or altered. Rather, the budget is explained with the concordance of a significant number of electors. An alliance such as this is formidable.

Perhaps the most obvious advantage to parents when school site budgeting is adopted is the linking of identification with the neighborhood school unit. Parents are invited and encouraged to participate in planning for the school's every activity. Their contributions are carefully reviewed and do in fact influence the school's operations. While engaged in the budget planning process, parents receive a lot of information about the school and the school district, improving their understanding of the inherent options and limitations of school expenditures. Appropriately, the information is presented in a clear and concise format and in small units, relating exclusively to a single school building. The positions that parents take are consequently based on an improved level of understanding. And, parents can trace their input throughout the process and can pin point the level where their suggestions were altered or abandoned and the rationale for such curtailments. That also lets parents know where an appeal process may commence. In all cases, the school site budgeting process provides a forum for focusing local interest on local school matters.

Parents also benefit from having their children's education matched to their unique needs. Classroom decisions are self generated, not imposed from a remote administrative level. There's also assurance that each pupil is being provided with equivalent shares of the instructional offerings of the school district. The built in process of achievement of district objectives reassures parents of the effectiveness of the school programs. Parents can learn of the scope and sequence of daily efforts to achieve the district's common objectives. Then too, parents are able to affect the district objectives to better fit community goals and aspirations.

While the connotation of integration has mostly been aimed at racial or language differences, an equally important element of socio-economic integration is fostered by school site budgeting. Equivalent resources are provided to each school enabling the acquisition of equally expert staffing ratios and equivalent access to books, materials, facilities, and instructional paraphernalia. All the schools of the district receive equivalent consideration.

With all available resources parcelled out to schools, a new confidence in public budgeting emerges. Suspicions of waste, duplicity, budget padding, holdbacks, or unplanned contingency funding are negated. The subsequent budgetary support is broadly based, informed, articulate, and convincing.

Business Services Office

The enlarged accounting system that is provoked by budget planning on a school site basis is a decided advantage in identifying and tracking cost elements. Such candid detail is not only readable for daily operations, it facilitates auditing and report requirements, and displays a lot of information for both long and short range planning assumptions. The central business office routines are elevated to an executive review function - with each school making independent fund allocations and expenditures, and being accountable for their activities. Conflicts are not generated by misinformation or a need for missing information. Each school unit is fully appraised of its fiscal circumstances. The essence of equal treatment and resource assignment is a responsibility that is removed from a central business office.

Schools will use assigned monies with improved effectiveness and efficiency. This takes place because of the self serving incentive of conservation and stretching of assigned resources. If an expenditure can be reduced, the funds saved can be applied to other building level needs. Coincidentally, if school unit expenditures exceed the allocation in an account, offsetting savings must be recouped from other accounts. Thus, the resources are precisely matched to the expenditure needs. Fiscal problems tend to be resolved at lower administrative levels, closer to those in a best position to evaluate their ramifications.

In conclusion, school site budgeting may be the most sensible approach to the perplexing fiscal problems of a school district. By its very nature of openness and the involvement of so many people, support emerges from within the school constituency. The flexibility of the planning process permits easy and prompt adjustment to the constraints and conditions dictated by fiscal, personnel, or community resources.

The leadship of middle managers is solicited, nurtured, and capitalized upon as they direct their budget planning communities to elevated deliberations. Budget reviewers cannot ignore the aggregation of public opinion reflected in such grass roots planning activity. The budgets for the schools of the district are responsive to the consumers rather than the bureaucrats. The result: a community that is turned on to school matters.

A 60 Second Test

Ask these questions when first considering school site budgeting .....

1. Is the superintendent fully committed to it?

2. Does the school board and the community want decentralized budgeting?

3. Are there any reservations about operating in a transparent vault?

4. Will middle managers respond?

5. Are labor relations stabilized?

6. Can broadly based parental participation be expected?

7. Does a highly competent business operation exist in the district?

8. Rank the following reasons for wanting school site budgeting:

   For Better Education
   For improved personnel decisions
   To decentralize administration
   For increased public support
   For meaningful staff participation
   To assure equality
   For improved planning
   To try a different approach
   To de-fuse budgeting
   As a better allocation process
   To provide flexibility
   To develop a better budget document
   To invigorate the schools
   To outflank political processes
   To promote better management
   To improve the image of the school board
   To provide more appropriate instructional materials
   It's democracy personified